TENNIS FOR ANYONE!

TENNIS
FOR ANYONE!

Sarah Palfrey

Foreword by Althea Gibson
Introduction by Gladys M. Heldman

CORNERSTONE LIBRARY   NEW YORK

CORNERSTONE LIBRARY PUBLICATIONS
Are Distributed By
Simon & Schuster Inc.
630 Fifth Avenue
New York, New York 10020

Manufactured in the United States of America
under the supervision of
Rolls Offset Printing Co. Inc. N. Y.

To

MAIA and GLADYS

*without whose encouragement this book
might never have been written*

ACKNOWLEDGMENTS

My thanks first to *World Tennis* magazine and to the United States Lawn Tennis Association, who have cooperated with me so willingly in regard to material and photographs for this book. They made my task a much more enjoyable one. I'd also like to thank my hundreds of tennis friends who have so enriched my life over the years. They have helped to write the book without being aware of it. So have many of my pupils. So have my tennis partners and opponents.

MY GRATITUDE

To my many newspaper and tennis writer friends in appreciation of all they have done for the game of tennis over the years, especially to Allison Danzig of *The New York Times* (no relation, but a dear friend), Al Laney of the *New York Herald Tribune*, Herbert Warren Wind of the *New Yorker*, and Peter Wilson of the London *Daily Mirror*, all of whom have contributed so much in the way of honest, fair and exciting reporting of tennis matches, and whose friendship over a period of more than twenty years I have valued beyond words.

To Mr. Edwin C. Baker and the staff of the USLTA.

To the many dedicated officials, linesmen, umpires, and referees of the various tennis associations, who have given so much of their lives to this great sport.

To my hosts and hostesses throughout the world who have let me live with them during tournaments, especially the late Julian Myricks, who became my second family away from home.

MY SPECIAL THANKS

To Gladys Heldman, who, in my opinion, has done more for tennis and tennis players in the last decade than any individual I know.

To Mrs. Wightman, who gave me such a wonderful boost in the beginning.

To my four sisters and one brother for the many years of practice and friendly rivalry.

To my husband, Jerry, who has been so patient and understanding during these past few months of writing.

S.P.

FOREWORD

Sarah Palfrey, friend of all tennis players, has been a friend of mine since 1949, when we first batted balls back and forth on Manhattan's East Side at the start of my big-time tournament career. She is a person of many talents, as I have discovered through our long association.

Sarah's all-around experience in tennis, as player, champion, and coach, truly qualifies her to show how tennis can be played and enjoyed by anyone who can hold a tennis racket. Her book, with its clear presentation of fundamentals and sound professional advice, offers a new outlook for any aspiring player, whether he wishes to be competitive or not. TENNIS FOR ANYONE! ought to be widely read. I am sure that it will be.

Althea Gibson

1957–58 United States Champion
1957–58 Wimbledon Champion
1960 World Professional Champion

INTRODUCTION

Sarah Palfrey has the same youth, charm, vivacity and keenness for tennis today as she had years ago, when she was a little girl making her first appearance in national tennis circles. She was a delight on the court as a youngster—sparkling, beautiful, graceful and always in good humor—and today when she appears on a court she appears just as sprightly and as talented. She has the same intelligent approach to the game, the same sound strokes and the same admirable qualities of sportsmanship. If ever a great player was to write a tennis book for young adults, it would have to be Sarah—for her understanding of the game, her vast experience in international competition and her continuing interest in the development of new, young talent.

Sarah was one of five Bostonian sisters, each of whom won one or more national titles. Polly Palfrey won the National Girls' Doubles in 1924. Lee Palfrey won the National Girls' Indoor Doubles in 1926; Mianne Palfrey won the National Girls' Doubles title three times both indoors and out (with Sarah) and took the singles once; and Joanna Palfrey was Girls' Indoor Doubles Champion with Sarah in 1930. But the most famous Palfrey of all was Sarah. She won the U. S. National Doubles title nine times with four different partners —with Betty Nuthall in 1930, with Helen Jacobs in 1932, 1934 and 1935, with Alice Marble in 1937, 1938, 1939 and 1940, and with Margaret Osborne in 1941. She was twice National Singles Champion, both times beating Pauline Betz in the final (1941 and 1945). She was four times National Mixed Doubles Champion—with Fred Perry, Enrique Maier, Don Budge and Jack Kramer. She teamed with Alice Marble to win the Wimbledon Doubles twice, and she was on every U. S. Wightman Cup team from 1930 through 1939!

But Sarah is not only one of the all-time greats; she is also a born teacher. She has the same analytical tennis brain as Jack Kramer and Maureen Connolly. She sees grips, footwork, strokes, speed, talent and, even more important, the desire of a player to improve or become great and the competitor qualities that make a champion. Sarah has always helped so many players—from young novices who have never before held a racket to champions-in-the-making, such as Althea Gibson—that I am glad she has finally decided to put down her wisdom in writing.

Gladys M. Heldman, Publisher
World Tennis Magazine

CONTENTS

1 · WHY TENNIS?

So you're thinking of learning how to play tennis but are not quite sure how to go about it, or even whether or not you'll be able to learn. Perhaps you are already a mediocre tennis player but want to be a better one. Or maybe you are an above-average player and have ambitions of becoming a champion. No matter what your present status or ambition, you have chosen the right sport, because tennis is without doubt the greatest game there is. It uses the best qualities of mind and body—it's sort of a combination chess-and-poker game on the tennis-court battlefield.

Besides being the greatest sport, tennis is the most enjoyable. No matter how good (or bad) you are, you should and will have fun out of tennis. In fact, I'll go so far as to predict that tennis can and will change your life, provided of course that you make some effort yourself.

How often I've met people in their twenties and thirties who say they wish they had learned the game in their teens. There is no question about it: the earlier you start, the easier it is to learn. The muscles are flexible; the mind is alert and uncluttered.

Unlike many sports, tennis is a game that you can play most of your life, if you are sensible about it. It would be difficult, for instance, to organize a friendly afternoon baseball, football or basketball game after you are through college. All Friday evening would be spent on the telephone making up the teams for a Saturday or Sunday, not to mention the time involved in arranging for an available field. For tennis all you need is one other player (or three others at the most, for doubles), a court, a racket and three balls. And only an hour of your valuable time.

Tennis used to be a game for the fortunate rich. Times have changed. Within the last thirty years it has become a game for practically anyone who wants to play. In fact today there are over eight million tennis players in the United States alone. What with more and more public and school courts sprouting up continually, to say nothing of the new bubble courts, indoor clay courts and all-weather courts, which you may rent by the hour, you're bound to find one in your area, even if you aren't lucky enough to belong to a club.

13

Just think of some of the benefits derived from tennis. Health and physical fitness are almost too obvious to mention. But what a pleasant way to do a portion of your calisthenics. Ask your doctor about it; I'm sure he'll agree that tennis helps develop muscles in all parts of the body without overdeveloping them, as do some other sports. Offhand, I can name three famous champions, Bill Tilden, Sidney Wood and Doris Hart, who were advised by their doctors to take up tennis in order to build up their stamina and weak muscles. Look what happened to them—they won at Wimbledon, no less.

Keeping youthful and attractive are two more benefits from playing tennis. Just glance around. You don't see many fat, flabby tennis players (as you do some golfers, for instance). Actors and actresses know this. Look at Ginger Rogers today. She hardly seems a year older than she did twenty years ago. Tennis is her favorite sport. So do Dina Merrill, Katharine Hepburn, Kirk Douglas, Mickey Rooney and Gilbert Roland, to name a few others.

Politicians also realize what tennis can do for them. Washington, D.C., is swarming with politicians, as well as diplomats, who are tennis enthusiasts. Adlai Stevenson was a devotee, and so was John F. Ken-

Many champions give a great deal of their time to encouraging young players, champions like Pauline Betz, Bill Talbert and Vic Seixas, to name a few. Pancho Gonzalez is shown here presenting trophies to the sixteen winners and runners-up at the first YMCA tennis clinic organized in Tuscaloosa.

nedy. In San Francisco during the 1964 Republican Presidential Convention, I didn't have much trouble persuading then-Congressman John V. Lindsay (later to become Mayor of New York City) to take an hour off from work to play with me and a couple of junior champions at the "Cal Club." Senator Javits had just finished playing as we arrived. John was as spry as a teenager and looked great, ready to go back to work afterwards with renewed energy.

Apart from these physical benefits, tennis does wonders for the mind, too. It helps build confidence, courage and imagination, which may be applied in other fields. My daughter, Diana, who was shy as a fifteen-year-old and never felt she was very good at anything, managed to win our junior club tournament at the Quaker Hill Country Club, in Pawling, New York. It was the first trophy she had ever won. Although she belittled her victory after the finals, saying that her opponent had had an off day and was really a better player, I am sure that this small win helped build Diana's confidence in herself, and that she was secretly very pleased.

You'll also find the tennis court a perfect place to forget your worries and problems. You'll be much too busy thinking about how and where

At the New York Central Park free tennis clinic, sponsored by the Eastern Tennis Patrons Association, the author teaches a group of beginners. *Photo by Max Peter Haas.*

to hit that small white ball to worry about why you got a C in History rather than a B. And learning to think quickly on the court can speed up your thinking in the classroom, or in the driver's seat, for instance.

Perhaps the greatest of all benefits to be gained from tennis is making friends. How quickly you make friends on a tennis court! Friends of all ages and types, either directly or indirectly. My friendships through tennis over the years have meant everything to me, not only in this country but throughout most of the world. Don't think that you have to be a champion, though, to make tennis friends. Just learn to play well enough so that you won't be a drag, and you'll be invited to play. Then one game leads to another . . . and on and on, far beyond the narrow confines of an actual court.

You may recall having read about the much-publicized romance between Crown Prince Akihito and lovely Michiko, who met while playing tennis on a court in Japan. It's a real Cinderella tale. He was immediately smitten, so the story goes, and now they are happily married. Their little Prince Hiro shows signs of being an athlete, judging from the pictures I have seen of him in the papers. I'm not promising that your games or matches will turn out as successfully as theirs, but you'll have fun whatever the results.

2 · HOW IT FEELS TO BE A BEGINNER

It's a rather strange yet exhilarating sensation to find yourself on a tennis court for the first time with a racket in your hand, seeing all that space around you and white lines going in different directions. For this very reason it is a good idea to begin tennis at an early age if possible. The younger you are, the less awkward you'll feel, and the more you will laugh at yourself when you fall flat on your derrière while chasing a backhand or lob.

At what age should one start? Actually there can be no accurate answer to this, because so much depends on the individual. The more natural ability and enthusiasm you have, the better. Height makes a difference, too—it helps if you're not too short. Many youngsters can start comfortably at eight or nine (my brother was enjoying it at five), while others have to wait a few more years. My son Jerry, at twelve, was just beginning to get fun out of the game. He had, however, played Ping-Pong and other ball games before, which helped train his eye.

Equipment

The first thing you'll need to begin playing is a tennis racket. It should be the best you can afford, and in order not to spend your money foolishly you should take along a "knowing" adult when you go shopping, or else get the advice of a good club pro. It's important to get the proper weight, balance, and handle for your age and size. All the well-known sporting-goods concerns carry good frames. Some are sturdier than others and will last longer; some are whippier or livelier than others but will warp sooner. Don't forget, in choosing your racket, that you must allow ¾ of an ounce for the gut. So if you buy a racket that weighs 12½ ounces unstrung, it will be 13¼ ounces strung. The average weight racket for a girl is from 13 to 13½ ounces strung; for a boy from 13½ to 14 ounces strung. Girls usually prefer lighter rackets with smaller handles. The main thing, however, is to select one that suits *you*: it must have a good "feel" as you swing it.

The gut in the racket, by the way, is just as important as the frame. I've seen so many beginners flourishing expensive rackets that they have

17

"At what age should one start?" My daughter Diana shows some interest at the age of two and a half. *Photo by Max Peter Haas.*

picked up at sales—strung with soft, mushy gut. No one can do justice to his game with a badly strung racket. The gut will do lots of the work for you, if you'll give it a chance. Another decision for you to make now concerning the stringing is whether to choose nylon or real gut (which is quite a bit more expensive, doesn't last as long, and frays or pops in wet weather). Obviously if you're a beginner (unless you're a millionaire), you won't think twice about choosing the nylon. But get a good grade of nylon and have it strung by a man who knows his business. If you can afford two rackets and are a good player, then you may splurge and get one of each: use the one with nylon for practice and in damp weather; and save your good one for matches and important occasions.

Keep your racket (or rackets) in a rubberized canvas case and a press whenever it's not in use, and it will give you many seasons of happy tennis-ing. Naturally, if you outgrow your racket, you'll have to buy another, but you can always pass down your first one to a younger friend or member of the family. You may even make a trade.

Prices for rackets run anywhere from ten to thirty dollars apiece. So you see there's a wide range to choose from. A good restringing job costs from five to nine dollars for nylon, depending on the quality of the nylon; and may go as high as fifteen dollars for high-grade or tournament gut.

Besides a racket, the other big expense is a supply of balls. Buy (or share) a can of balls as often as you can, because it's hard to control the balls when they become light and the fuzz wears off. The cost for a can of three varies from $1.80 to $2.75. Keep an eye out for store sales; and remember you can buy good used balls at sanctioned tournaments.

Now you've got a racket and balls. All you need is wearing apparel (see page 74) which should be comfortable and white (although colored trims are now acceptable and attractive), a good pair of flat, rubber-soled sneakers, a hat or sun visor in hot weather, and a tennis glove, if your hand slips a lot.

The most important matter when you start actually playing, whether you're ten or twenty, is to find someone to show you how to hold the racket correctly. This helps you to avoid all sorts of bad habits, which are so hard to undo later. (The proper grips are shown in detail in a later chapter.)

Watch . . . and Practice

Another fine idea for a beginner is to watch the good players whenever possible, either in tournaments or practice. It's amazing how much you can learn by watching. The trick here is *not* to watch the ball after it has been hit, but to keep your eye on the player himself, watching his strokes, movements, footwork and court positions. Notice how the good player will start moving for the next shot the second the ball leaves his racket, while the poorer player will pause a bit to see where his own shot is going, thus wasting precious "getting-back-into-position" seconds.

At the Longwood Cricket Club, our home club in Chestnut Hill, Massachusetts, my four sisters, Polly, Lee, Mianne, Joanna, our brother John, and I used to attend all the big tournaments held at the club. And they were important tournaments: the National Doubles, the Longwood Bowl, and the Massachusetts State. There we followed our favorite heroes from court to court in awe, players like Bill Tilden, Billy Johnston, Helen Wills, Molla Mallory, and the great foreign players who came from overseas to play in the National Doubles. From these champions we learned a tremendous amount. After watching them all afternoon, we'd rush home to the court on our farm in the country and play until darkness, trying to imitate them as best we could.

We realized how lucky we were to have a court of our own to play on from spring to fall. It was a clay court, and we had to take care of it by ourselves, doing all the watering, rolling and laying-down of the tapes. We also had the advantage of ready-made, eager opponents day in and day out, each one trying to beat the other. To prove what a great boon this was, all five of us sisters had won National Junior titles by the time we were eighteen.

Polly, the oldest (who now has a daughter of her own), won the National Junior Girls' Doubles with Fanny Curtis; Lee, the second oldest (now the mother of two daughters), won the National Junior Indoor Doubles with Marjorie Morrill; Mianne, the third sister (now the mother of five), won the National Junior Doubles and the National Junior Indoor Doubles three times each with her next younger sister (me), as well as the National Women's Indoor Singles, once; and the fifth sister, Joanna (she now has four children), won the National Junior Indoor Doubles with me. Our only brother, John, the youngest member of the family, won a couple of Massachusetts State Junior Doubles titles, but was too busy with more important pursuits to give tennis his full attention. We all agree that he could have won a national title if he had seriously tried.

Most beginners aren't so fortunate and have to scurry around to find their opponents and courts. It's not terrifically difficult, but it does take time. If possible, find an opponent who is better than you, even if you have to give him or her frequent home-cooked meals or tickets to the movies. Use your ingenuity; it will be worth it. If you play against someone as bad as you are in the beginning, neither one of you will improve much, because the ball will seldom be returned.

The best method to start, if you are really a beginner, is to cajole a parent, relative or close friend to toss the balls to you underhand. He, or she, will stand near the net on the same side as you (who will be in the middle of the court on the base line) and throw you a few easy forehands, which you won't be made to reach for at first; then a few easy backhands, also within easy reach; then alternate shots, first forehand, next backhand and then forehand again. In this way you will get loads of shots to hit and will soon acquire a sense of timing and a feel for the ball, without worrying about footwork—yet.

Do be nice to your helper afterwards, because it's pretty boring work. If you can afford a professional, so much the better. He *has* to help you; he's being paid for it. And his help will pay off for you.

I remember coaching a nine-year-old boy in Key West, Florida, who showed absolutely no sign of coordination. After four lessons I came as close as I ever have to giving up. The boy wasn't making any connection between the racket and ball, even when I was gently tossing balls right to him. He was suffering, and so was I. However I decided to try a little longer. Suddenly, during the sixth session, he made contact with two balls in a row. You should have seen his face light up! He

Tennis is getting to be more and more of a family game. Here are the Julius Heldmans of New York City, now living in Houston, Texas, who have no trouble finding a partner or opponent. Gladys took up the game *after* the birth of her two daughters. Julius was a National Junior champion in 1936 and twice National Senior Indoor champ in 1964 and 1965. Julie M. (holding Putty the cat) was National Junior Girls Singles Champion in 1963 and has twice been ranked No. 2 woman player in the United States in 1968 and 1969. Julie is now one of the top players of the Women's Pro Tour. Carrie is a fine social player in her own right.

grinned a real, genuine grin for the first time. From then on we were on our way. His mother told me weeks later that his new-found interest in tennis had made a different boy out of him both at home and at school. He was no longer afraid to take his turn at bat, throw a football, try a dance step or even make new friends.

Aids to Practice

Another suggestion for you right now is to do just what you're doing: read a book. This gives you time to think things over at your leisure without being rushed and confused on the court. I shall never forget my older sister Lee's experience with Bill Tilden's book. At the age of twelve, she had borrowed it from a friend, and her nose was buried in it for days. It meant everything to her, not only for what it said, but because it had been written by Tilden, her idol. Dreading the day when she would have to return it, she began to copy it all out in longhand, painfully, slowly, word for word. Our mother and father were so amused when they discovered what was going on behind the closed bedroom door that they mentioned the story to some friends at a dinner party (Lee by this time was about a third of the way through). The friends happened to know a friend of Tilden's—and so, we later discovered, it all got back to Tilden himself. A week later, with no warning, a package arrived by mail for Lee. It was an autographed copy of The Book! It said, "To Lee Palfrey, who was kind enough to care to copy my book. Bill Tilden." Lee, of course, walked on air— and the rest of us were touched with reflected glory.

As a sequel to this story, in four years, when I was twelve, I helped Bill Tilden lose the semifinal round of the mixed doubles in a senior grass-court tournament at the Agawam Hunt Club in Rhode Island. However, we became firm friends thereafter; and he helped me with my game many times in the years that followed.

Reading in itself doesn't do much good, though, if you don't practice what you're reading about. A good idea at this stage is to find a practice wall or backboard, against which you can practice hitting balls to yourself. Many clubs have these. (They should, even if they don't.) If you don't belong to a club, there are other substitutes: a handball court in the park; the wall of a school gym when not in use; even a garage door. All that is needed are a flat surface (with room enough to swing) and a backstop.

Practice makes champions. Peaches Barkowitz has hit 950 volleys in a row off a wall, and 1775 times off a wall on one bounce, according to her late coach, Mrs. Jean Hoxie. Here is Peaches as a youngster, hitting a not-too-hard forehand drive. *World Tennis Magazine.*

Many schools and colleges allow their gyms to be used for this purpose at certain times of day. At Barnard College in New York City, I looked in at an afternoon tennis session recently, and the physical education teacher was doing a remarkable job of coaching eight to ten players at a time during a half-hour period in the big gym.

Althea Gibson started her brilliant tennis career by playing paddle tennis on a Police Athletic League play street in Harlem. She was the champion of the block. This led to learning regular tennis on a handball court with two secondhand rackets given to her by a friend, bandleader Buddy Walker, who thought she showed unusual ability. This, in turn, led to her playing on a real court.

I used to practice against a twelve-foot space of brick wall in back of our house in Brookline. The ground was too uneven for the ball to bounce, so I had to hit all shots on the fly. This must have helped me to become a good volleyer and doubles player, since volleying became the best part of my game. After paying for too many broken windows, my parents decided it would be less expensive to have a wooden wall nailed to the inside of the far end of our garage. We sisters painted a white line the height of a tennis net and practiced happily, even in winter time. Why our neighbors didn't complain about the noise I'll never understand.

Outside the Harlem tenement where Althea Gibson's family lived and where she first played paddle tennis. *Photo by Max Peter Haas.*

One advantage of practicing by yourself is that you escape the embarrassment of looking foolish in front of others when you try frantically to make contact with the ball. For some of you, though, who may have slow reflexes, a practice board is too fast, and is definitely not for you. The ball comes off the wall much too quickly and won't give you enough time to get set. You can graduate to it later on.

There is on the market a fine commercial practice net which may be adjusted to regulate the speed of the rebounding ball. There is also a fancy tennis-ball machine that shoots balls out to you at various speeds at regulated intervals, a kind of "robot-professional." These two items are expensive for an individual to own. They are ideal for a club or school, however. (See the section on "Useful Information.")

Types of Courts

As you probably know, there are different types of courts throughout the country. In the East one is apt to find grass, clay, composition, and wood courts (in indoor armories). Grass courts favor the aggressive player, because the ball bounces fast and low, making it easy for

A tennis-ball machine shoots the balls out at regulated speeds. *Frann Studios.*

a good server and volleyer to put the shot away. Clay courts on the other hand favor the speedy retriever, because the ball bounces slower and higher, giving him more time to get to the ball. The slower the clay court the more difficult it is to put a volley away.

Composition courts are somewhere in between grass and clay: the ball bounces higher than on grass and faster than on clay. It's a very good surface that is growing in popularity and requires little upkeep.

Wood courts, more than any other surface, really favor the "big" serve and volley. The ball shoots and skids by so fast that a player needs very quick reflexes, hardly any backswing, and 20-20 vision.

In the Far West you find hardly any courts that are not cement or asphalt (like Grasstex). These courts favor the aggressive player, since the ball bounces fast and high. (You'd better get a good pair of tennis shoes: these courts can be rough on the feet.)

The South has more clay courts than any other kind. So does the Middle West. But more and more you will find more new composition courts being built in all parts of the country. Hard courts made of different synthetic materials like Dynaturf, Elastaturf and Uni-Turf can be tailored for fast or slow play. Special coatings like Plexipave

Tennis in New York City. The Tennis Center has three excellent courts on the roof of a building on Thirty-eighth Street facing the Chrysler Building.

are very satisfactory over any flat surface. Then there are increasingly popular acrylic carpet coverings like Sportface that play quite a lot like grass courts, which of course are slowly dying out due to their expensive upkeep.

The type of court you play on right now is not your chief worry at the moment, however. Your project is to find *any* court. See if you can't find a friend who knows a friend who has a court. Or scout the public parks and schools in your area.

No matter how you start, the main thing is not to get discouraged when you don't improve as fast as you think you should or when you fan ten shots in a row. You will find that the few good shots you make as time goes on will more than compensate for the many bad ones. The only times you should feel discouraged are when you give up too easily or when you're too lazy to try. If this happens, you should sit down and have a fight-talk with yourself—not about tennis, but about *you.*

3 · WHAT HAVE YOU GOT?

Take Advantage of Natural Abilities

Let's face it. Some of us have more ability than others. First of all you should take a good look in the mirror; not to admire, but to analyze yourself and see what you've got. This book was written to help you utilize it and decide what sort of tennis style is best suited to your physical and mental makeup. You have a body—for better or for worse, the only one you'll have. It's up to you to decide how you're going to use it.

You may happen to be a boy of fifteen, let's say, who grew eight inches in the last two years and is now six feet tall, and you feel as though you have two left feet—always stumbling and tripping over them. Don't despair. You'll get over it; and much sooner than you think. Actually tennis will help you do it. There are ways to move and take steps (which I'll describe in the chapter on strokes) that will make you less clumsy.

The best thing for you to work on at this time is your serve. Being tall will give you a big advantage over the little fellow, and you are in a position to develop a really powerful serve right now. But—don't let power go to your head and try to crack every ball for an ace. Remember that consistency is better than an occasional placement (an old cliché perhaps, but a true one). Of course service aces are gallery pleasers and ego satisfiers, and, if you have a girl friend on the sidelines, you would no doubt impress her with flashes of brilliant aces. But I wouldn't like to see her expression after a series of double faults. Far better some solid serves with an occasional ace thrown in for an extra thrill.

Besides putting extra emphasis on your serve, you should also make considerable effort with your volleying (hitting the ball in the air before it bounces). These two, serving and volleying, go hand in hand. If your serve is strong enough, you will be apt to get a weak return from your opponent, which you will have a good chance of putting away with a volley up at the net (provided that you can get there without tripping over your feet on the way).

By emphasizing the serve and volley, I don't mean to imply that you should neglect your ground strokes entirely. Of course, you shouldn't: you should keep working at them. I only mean that, until you get more accustomed to your newly acquired height and long legs, it will be very difficult for you to get too many shots off the ground. You should instead make the most of what is easiest for you in order to enjoy yourself during the growing period.

How about a player who is not tall? Let's take a completely different situation. This time the body is short and stocky and belongs to a girl. You are she, and you are good at basketball (I could have said track, swimming, baseball, or any of the team games). You don't meet many boys on the basketball court, though, and you are discovering that you'd like to—they're not as bad as you used to think. Tennis is the perfect sport for you. Since you're athletic to begin with, you'll be able to learn tennis more quickly than the average person. Before expecting to be invited to play, however, you must be good enough not to be a bore (or a handicap, if you're playing doubles); at least be able to put your service into play and hit some returns over the net.

Being short, you can't expect to become as powerful a hitter or develop such an aggressive game as your taller friends. You should concentrate on good, steady, well-placed ground strokes plus speedy footwork, the way Pauline Betz and Chuck McKinley, two of the fleetest I ever saw, used to do. Here's where your ability in basketball or track will give you a big advantage in tennis: you will be able to cover the court so fast that you will get to your opponents' best shots and eventually wear them down and cause errors. This was the method used so successfully by Bobby Riggs and Bitsy Grant against the big champions like Don Budge and Ellsworth Vines. The players were glaringly mismatched as to size, but in no other way, as some startling upsets proved, especially on clay courts, which allowed more time to chase the balls.

Here again I don't want to imply that you should neglect your serve. But since it's not going to be the main part of your game (because you don't have the power), you can use it as a useful and necessary tool to set up the part of your game that is your forte—your ground strokes. Your best bet is to develop a low, well-placed serve that will not give your opponent a chance to force you too much on the return.

Don't try to learn an American twist serve if you're short. I discovered this sad fact the hard way: I tried it. All 5 feet 3 of me tried it. It looked so great when I watched Alice Marble, Louise Brough, Doris Hart, Neale Fraser, or Rod Laver make the ball take a terrific hop and pull the opponent way out of court, especially on the backhand side. It wasn't very difficult to learn a fairly reasonable facsimile of their serves; with six months of constant practice, the hop was getting hoppier, much to my delight. What I hadn't realized was that, because I was learning it on cement courts in California, it looked better than it really was. My rude awakening to its true value took place in the mixed doubles finals of the National Clay Court Championships in River Forest, Illinois. Elwood Cooke and I were playing against Pauline Betz and Pancho Segura. Unlike most mixed doubles formations, where the girl (being the weaker of the two) plays in the right-hand court, and the man plays in the left, Betz and Segura shifted the arrangement, since Pauline had probably the greatest backhand in women's tennis, and Pancho had probably the greatest two-fisted forehand in the game. You've really missed something if you haven't seen this shot. Therefore when I was serving from my right court into the forehand court, it was to Pancho's strong side. Try as I would, it was

Pancho Segura of Ecuador, who became one of the top-ranking players of the United States, has probably the greatest two-fisted forehand in the game. He's still going strong as a professional.

an impossibilty for me to get a serve onto his backhand. My supposedly high-bouncing American twist, which was intended for his backhand, didn't have enough power on the slower clay court and he had plenty of time to run around his backhand and wallop it, with his two-fisted "Big Bertha," right down my throat (my tummy to be more exact), as I was following my serve in to the net. Needless to say it didn't take me long to go back to my old, reliable, low-bounding slice. (P.S.: We finally squeezed out the match.)

At least I've saved you the time and energy of having to find out for yourself. Leave the big serve to the big fellow. You can still get up to the net to volley, though, but not often on your serve, and you'll have to wait longer and be more choosy as to the running-in shot. Being quick, you will have no trouble getting to the net on time the minute you see a short shot coming. Of course you must watch out for lobs over your head. You can't crowd the net too closely, and you must learn a half volley and a good low volley, since you'll be getting many balls at your feet.

What happens when you're not particularly athletic but are quite talented at ballet or other kinds of dancing and/or figure skating? You are lucky in many ways. You are bound to have good rhythm and timing, two essentials for good tennis, plus a third extremely important attribute, not always understood—balance. You are blessed if you have one or all three of these qualities (they usually go together). You will find tennis not only easy to learn without going through the awkward stages of those less fortunately endowed, but you will also get great enjoyment out of the sheer motion of hitting the ball and moving smoothly over the surface of the court. I doubt that you will ever be a tiger or care one way or another about winning matches. That won't be your purpose.

If you're a good swimmer and diver, you can also be a good tennis player. Here again rhythm and timing will be invaluable. So will your coordination. And swimming and tennis go together so naturally—like bacon and eggs. There is nothing more refreshing than a cool swim after a lively game of tennis!

Getting back to coordination for a minute, what a fine attribute this is to have . . . when one part of the body seems to know instinctively what another part is doing, or even what it is going to do. The brain sends messages so fast you don't realize they're being sent. Good coordination is essential for quick reflexes, which in turn are essential for good tennis. I can best describe a person with quick reflexes as one who, when he drops a wet cake of soap in the shower, can catch it before it lands on the floor. Obviously this is something you can't practice—it just happens unexpectedly and automatically, without thought. Coordination is, therefore, a God-given gift. Althea Gibson, the great Negro tennis star, once said to me, "Sarah, we're lucky. I know I'm lucky. I'm not boasting but I know God gave me this gift of ability and coordination for some reason, and if I didn't use it, I'd be doing Him a disfavor. That's why I wanted so much to be a tennis champion. Now, having achieved that goal, I want to be a golf champion."

It's a funny thing about golf and tennis. Almost every good tennis player I know who has taken up golf in later years, and who has really worked at it, has become a good golfer. Ellsworth Vines, after retiring from tennis, got to the semifinals of the U.S. National Amateur Golf Championship before turning professional, and has been a very successful teaching one ever since. Other tennis players, like Bobby Riggs, Elwood Cooke, Frank Guernsey, Roy Emerson, Pauline Betz, Alice Marble and many others, have become really good golfers.

It doesn't seem to work in reverse, though. I don't happen to know any good golfers who have become good tennis players, with the possible exception of some who learned tennis when they were young. The only person to my knowledge who ever got to the finals of both the National Golf and Tennis Championships was that remarkable lady Mary K. Browne, who won the golf title once and was in the finals of the tennis twice. But she didn't take up tennis *after giving up* golf . . . which is my point: she learned and played them simultaneously. (She would be an exception in anybody's book anyway, regardless of the details: truly an extraordinary talent.) But golfers as a rule just don't make good tennis players. Veteran golfers must lack the special ability to deal with the moving ball, because certainly timing and coordination are equally important for both sports.

Baseball players are naturals for tennis. I know quite a few well-known ones personally. Hank Greenberg, for instance, has become an excellent tennis player since stepping down from big-time baseball.

It does seem to apply that if you're good at one sport you're apt to be good at most other sports, including tennis, if you know how to go about it.

Most of what we've been discussing, however, has had to do with the physical aspects of "What You've Got." This is only half of tennis, if you want to get the most fun out of it. Just as important is what you've got in your head that can be put to good use. You should take stock of yourself and analyze your mentality, so that your whole character can play a part in the kind of tennis you want to play. Are you cautious, methodical; or daring and imaginative? These are the matters of personality that will make a big difference in your type of game. There is more on strategy and temperament in the chapters on competition.

Here are four former tennis champs, who have taken up golf and become experts. From left to right: Dick Savitt, Don Budge, Ellsworth Vines and Bobby Riggs, who is putting at the Inwood Country Club, Long Island, where Vines was the pro. *Inwood News Photo Service.*

4 · WHAT DO YOU LACK?

By now I hope you have thought of a few assets that you've got, both physical and mental. But while hunting for these, you no doubt kept bumping into realizations of things that you lack—like strong wrists, a sense of timing, confidence and control of temper, to mention a few.

Believe it or not, tennis can do wonders for all of these lacks. Tennis actually strengthens weak wrists; develops timing and confidence; and certainly helps relieve overheated tempers. Just get that body of yours overheated for a few minutes chasing drop shots and lobs: then see how the temper miraculously cools off, even as you wipe your brow.

The Law of Compensation

There are always ways of counteracting a deficiency in one area by making more of something else. Take Helen Wills, for instance. You've surely heard of her even if you never saw her play. Her forte was her powerful serve, along with magnificent ground strokes (plus a few other advantages—like nerves of steel and hardly ever making an error). But she wasn't much of a volleyer, and she knew it. Her reflexes were a trifle slow, as was her footwork. She was plenty fast in singles, when she had more time, but not in doubles. She could run endlessly sideways along the base line but had trouble getting up to the net on time, in moving forward and back quickly, which you have to do in top-flight doubles. Yet she enjoyed doubles so much! (She still does, as a matter of fact.)

What did she do to compensate for her lack of speed in getting to the net? She developed a great lob and became one of the best lobbers I've ever seen. When she didn't have time to get to the net, she would stay in the back court and alternate her powerful drives with her well-placed lobs, both cunningly disguised, of course. Her looping back swing, the same for both, made it almost impossible for her opponent to tell what was coming. Her partner would scuttle around all over the forecourt and take care of all the short shots, his and hers. You can see for yourself why she needed a first-rate, sprightly volleyer for a partner. This she realized; and, being Queen Helen, she always arranged for it (part of the game, you know).

33

The great Helen Wills, who was in her prime in the 1920s, reaches for a high backhand volley. *United States Lawn Tennis Association.*

The results of her smart thinking paid off: her doubles record speaks for itself. She won the National Mixed Doubles twice and the National Women's Doubles four times . . . not bad for a not-great volleyer or doubles player. On top of this she had enormous fun doing it. Choosing the right doubles partner can be very important, whether you want to win or not.

Here is where we get back to you. How do you know what sort of a doubles partner would be good for you? And how do you go about "capturing" him or her?

The Right Partner

Temperament plays a big part in the selection of a tennis partner, just as it does in any field—ballet, figure skating, the theater, dancing the frug, etc. Those making up the best teams seem to be suited to each other. You sense a certain rapport when you see Alfred Lunt and Lynn Fontanne, Rudolf Nureyev and Margot Fonteyn, Mr. and Mrs. Ely Culbertson . . . these great performers always seem (or seemed) to understand each other and to enjoy whatever it is they're doing. This rapport would apply to partners of the same sex also: Laurel and Hardy; Lucille Ball and Vivian Vance; or Alice Marble and me (we didn't lose one match in our four years of playing together).

It's important to you to find someone who will be fun to play with, who will be looking for the same pleasures out of the game that you are, who will complement you both tennis-wise and temperament-wise. Can you imagine pairing Phyllis Diller with Charles de Gaulle on the tennis court? In other words it would be downright silly for you to choose a partner who takes his game terribly seriously, when you just want to play for fun. It would put an immediate damper on what might have been a good friendship. He would glare at you when you made errors or didn't try hard enough (in his estimation), while you would be wishing that he'd just relax and enjoy himself.

On the other hand, if you are competitive and want to play seriously, your partner must be like you. You'll be working with a common purpose and a real team might develop both on and off the court.

There are other factors of temperament to be considered. Sometimes a person with an erratic disposition, who blows up when things go wrong, needs a partner who is a steadying influence and can calm his edgy nerves. Two overemotional players on the same side of the net could start a real conflagration. With many of the best teams, you'll find that one of the partners is apt to be the brilliant, high-strung type, and the other will be the steady, composed one, whom nothing bothers.

A sense of humor is almost a requisite in a satisfactory doubles partner (unless you don't have one yourself, in which case you both deserve each other—and heaven help you). So many odd, unexpected things happen on a tennis court. If you don't see the comical side, you're missing half the fun. I don't mean in an important tournament or an international match, when so much depends on the results and everyone is tense, although even then there is sometimes room for humor. I'm talking about the day-in-and-day-out matches, when you hit your partner on the back of the head with your second serve; when a dog tears

across the court at set-point; when your big romance of the moment
swings with full force to put away an overhead smash and misses the
ball entirely; when your bra strap or the elastic on your shorts breaks
in the middle of a rally. Happenings like these aren't rare at all: they
occur in almost every game or set you play. How can anyone help but
be amused?

So choose your partner with care as to temperament. Don't forget,
either, that you should give strong consideration to his tennis game,
because he may be able to provide something that you're missing.

Once you have decided upon the kind of partner you'd like to play
with . . . how do you find him or her? It looks easy on paper, you
say, but what's the next move? For a start, keep your eyes open, your
mind alert, and go on a search. Go to the local school, public, or club
courts and make yourself available to fill in as a fourth for practice
games. Try to pick out players about your own speed. If you're any
good, you'll be asked again: if not, you'd better go back to the practice
board or take more lessons.

There is no set rule or special etiquette about acquiring a doubles
partner. Anyone has a right to ask anyone else to play with him. Even
in tournaments this is true. Only in Davis Cup or Wightman Cup
matches, when you're representing your country, are you told with
whom you are to play. Otherwise it's catch-as-catch-can—or first come,
first served. Certainly with boys' and girls' doubles teams there should
be no shyness about asking someone to play with you. In mixed doubles, of course, there may be. For a girl to ask a boy may seem too
pushy (not the other way around, though). But with a dash of subtlety
she can surely get the point across that she would like him as a partner.
Subtlety like, "Oh, Jerry, that was such a good match you had this
afternoon! I watched every point. How did you ever get a serve like
that? Gosh, I'd give anything for even a halfway decent serve. It's my
big weakness. Do you think you could ever find time to give me some
help with mine? You would?" etc., etc. So a new team is formed. Not
too difficult if you go about it the right way.

The Right Opponent

As important as picking the right partner for doubles is the challenge of selecting a suitable opponent for singles, one who won't mag-

nify your deficiencies. If you're short-winded and tire easily, don't select an opponent who "poops" the ball back endlessly in long, tiring rallies. Choose one instead who makes enough errors to give you time to catch your breath. If you are very nearsighted and must wear glasses, don't choose an opponent who hits such a fast ball that he doesn't give you time to adjust your sights.

These examples are only meant to give you an idea of what you can do. You will discover, as you play along, that volleying is excellent for strengthening the wrists, that practice develops confidence and timing. In the chapter on fitness you will get more ideas on how to build up your body. You must learn how to apply your own solutions to your particular problems. The main thing to remember is that, whether you're playing singles or doubles, you can make up for what you lack by using something else you've got . . . most of all, your head.

5 · THE BASIC STROKES

No two people agree exactly as to how the different fundamental strokes are made; and no two people hit their shots in exactly the same way. But there are certain basic principles which *are* generally agreed upon.

The simplest style is best, from every point of view. It is the most effective; it's the easiest to learn; it depends less than others on natural ability; and, once you've learned it, you'll never forget it. In other words, you won't have the recurring "off days" that are the bane of many fancy-looking players, days when nothing is working for them.

I speak from bitter experience, since I was one of those so-called fancy players myself. For many years I was complimented on my pretty, graceful strokes, and when I had a good day everything went serenely. But things might suddenly go very wrong and I didn't really understand why. The trouble was that I had never worked diligently at my strokes or taken the time to analyze them. (In all fairness to myself, it was difficult during the long cold winters in Boston, when I could only play one hour on Saturday mornings indoors, to really work on my strokes . . . and springs and summers were filled with tournaments.) Be that as it may, I was more interested in where to put the ball, in tactics, than I was in strokes—an oversight that I was to regret later. Obviously the two should go together.

Finally I saw the light of day and really worked on my strokes; but I would have saved much grief and many lost matches if I had learned my strokes correctly in the first place. So be warned by my experience and believe me: it's much more difficult to undo something you've done wrong than to do it right in the beginning.

The following directions apply to a right-handed player. If you are left-handed, simply switch the terms and substitute "left" for "right" throughout. Your forehand will be on your left side, your backhand on your right.

THE FOREHAND DRIVE

Let's start with the *forehand drive,* the stroke that is probably used more often than any other. It should be developed into a steady, aggressive weapon which can act as the mainstay of your game—not to the exclusion of the other strokes, of course: the day is long past when, with a glaring weakness in your game, you could win a match of any consequence. But the forehand should be the foundation on which your game is built (along with the serve).

Fortunately most beginners find the forehand the most natural shot to start with—although they very seldom hit it right. First comes the question of the grip. There are three forehand grips, the Continental, the Eastern, and the Western. The Eastern is the one I recommend: it's a compromise between the more extreme positions, and it has proved the most suitable for any kind of surface. Almost all the champions with really great forehands have used the Eastern grip, including players like Bill Tilden, Ellsworth Vines, Jack Kramer, Helen Wills, Alice Marble, and Maureen Connolly. It is true that the current crop of wonderful Australian men players do use the Continental grip, and so did Fred Perry, the great English star, but to be successful with this grip, one needs a very strong wrist, perfect timing, and correct wrist motion. The combination is not too easy to come by. Besides, I can't thing of one Continental-grip user who has controlled power in his forehand to compare with that of Tilden, Vines, Kramer or Gonzalez. Flashy and spectacular, yes, but risky and erratic as well. Furthermore, the Eastern grip is the easiest to learn.

The usual method of describing the Eastern grip (you've probably heard it many times) is to say, "Hold out your hand and pretend you are going to shake hands with the racket." This may appeal to you. (Take hold of a racket and try it.) If not, here is a way I've had good luck with in helping young people.

Extend your right arm out to your side, about waist high, without your racket, and pretend you are going to hit the ball with the palm of your hand (as in handball). Then place the racket in your hand, without changing its position, wrapping your fingers around the handle just barely above, or just touching, the leather butt. Now imagine that the racket is just an extension of your arm. This should feel comfortable; you may want to shift your grip slightly until it does, because people's hands differ somewhat in size and shape. The fingers should hold the racket not too tightly or too loosely, but firmly. The forefinger may be extended a little up the handle to give you more flexibility and control.

The Continental grip (A): Grasp the handle between the thumb and the first finger, on the flat side of the racket; then close hand over the handle. This grip can be used for forehand or backhand. *The Western grip (B):* Grasp the handle with the V of the hand (between the thumb and the first finger) on the flat side of the handle. The forehand and the backhand are hit with the same side of the racket. This grip is rarely used today. *The Eastern grip (C–F):* Pretend you are going to hit the ball with the palm of your hand. Then, without changing position, place the racket in your hand, wrapping your fingers around the handle just barely above or just touching the leather butt.

This is your forehand grip. Now for the shot. To get into the ready position, face the net, crouching slightly, with your feet placed comfortably apart (not anchored, please—but ready to spring). This will

allow you to move quickly in any of six directions. You may count
them if you wish: left, right, forward, backward, up, and down; and
I suppose you might add diagonal. The throat of your racket (or just
below) is resting in your left hand, ready for a quick change of grip,
and your gaze is firmly *fixed on the ball*. Once you see that it is going
to land on your right side for a forehand drive, there are two things that
you must do simultaneously as one movement. First take your racket
straight back with your right arm, about waist high, as though you
were going to hit the ball with your bare hand. This should automatically turn your shoulders and hips sideways to the net. Practice this in
front of a mirror to see what I mean—you don't even need a racket to
get the idea. As you do this, take a step with your *right* foot, resting
on it slightly but not with full weight. Your left arm acts as a balance;
the right, hitting arm is extended comfortably back, neither stretching
nor cramped. The elbow is kept away from the body.

You are now ready to swing forward. *Don't be afraid to swing
freely!* Practice a few times without the ball until it begins to feel natural. Allow plenty of room. As you swing forward, step forward onto
your left foot, thus transferring your weight from the right foot to the
left. Try to meet the ball in front of you, on a line with your front foot
(the left one) as your weight is being transferred, so that you will put
the weight of your whole body into the ball instead of using just the
arm. This is the secret of power: weight transference at the right time.
It is the reason why some players seem to get so much power out of a
shot with so little effort, and it's therefore especially important for a
small person, who must make the most of all the strength he has.

As you swing forward for a waist-high flat drive, follow the horizon-
tal plane on which you took the racket back. For a higher bounce
swing the racket back on a higher level and follow through correspond-
ingly; for a lower bounce, the same thing on a lower level; and of
course for a very low ball you must bend your knees way down. On
the very high ones you have to decide whether to hit the ball on the
rise before it reaches the top of the bounce, to hit it overhand, or to
hit it at a comfortable height on its way down, which may be back at
the fence.

At the point of impact, the face of the racket should *be flat against*

the ball, tilted neither up nor down. This is very important. And so is
something else: the ball should be hit in the *middle of the gut.*

You will point the direction of the ball by the follow-through of the
racket and by the position of your feet, which should be more or less
parallel to the intended flight of the ball. Remember, as you follow
through, really to *hit through the ball,* almost as though you were going
to throw your racket out after it. If the production of the shot has been
correct so far, the racket then comes up of its own accord and ends its
course near your left shoulder, imparting very slight top spin to the
ball.

That's all. You have just finished a forehand drive. But that was
easy because, in the situation I just described, you didn't have to run
for the ball. Needless to say this doesn't happen in actual play. So
the next thing to consider is the footwork for the forehand—when you
have to move, and more often run, for the ball.

Footwork

One secret is this: the moment you see you are going to hit a forehand, start running with your *right* foot, no matter whether you're
heading forward, backward, or sideways. Then when you reach the

(Left) The author in the ready position—feet apart, knees slightly bent, ready to
spring in any direction. The racket rests in the left hand for quick change of grip.
(Right) Nancy Richey Gunter, the United States No. 1 ranking woman player in
1964, 1966, 1968 and 1969, hits a flat, solid forehand drive. Her left arm acts as a
balance during the back swing. She is about to step forward onto her left foot as
she swings through the ball, thus transferring her weight from the right to the left
foot. *World Tennis Magazine.*

Manuel Santana of Spain, the winner of the 1965 United States National Men's Singles Championship, has just finished a forehand drive. The racket has come up of its own accord with a good follow-through. He has kept his balance and will be able to get ready for the next shot.

ball, make sure that your weight is again slightly on the right foot, so that you can shift to the left foot as you make your forward swing. Another secret is to start taking your racket back *the instant you start to run,* so that all you have to do when you reach the ball is to swing forward. You will thus eliminate a lot of the last-minute, off-balance scramble that often takes place: you will be ready and waiting instead.

I can give you a few other hints about footwork. The best way to run is on the balls of your feet—not on your heels, of course, but not up on your tiptoes either. I used to dance around on tiptoes myself (I remember how my father teased me because the newspapers sometimes referred to me as "Little Miss Twinkle Toes"). And I suffered for it: I actually injured the bone joints of my two big toes, and wasted a great deal of energy besides. You can be just as quick running on the balls of your feet, quicker, in fact, as Bobby Riggs illustrated with his humorous duck-walk. Although he seemed to be running on his heels at times, they were actually just off the ground. He was one of the fastest and most effortless court coverers in tennis. And watch some of the current champs, Manuel Santana, Roy Emerson, Arthur Ashe and Dennis Ralston, for instance. They all run, skip or slide, as the case may call for, on the balls of their feet.

Take comfortably small steps and keep them as small as possible, because jerkiness produces bad timing and pulling up on your shots. Try to reserve your strength by taking only the necessary number of steps. Some players look so spectacular and athletic as they tear around the court, leaping and rushing in all directions. Actually they're wasting their energy. The best players anticipate so well and have such forceful shots that they don't need to leap and cavort: they are already there.

If you have judged the ball correctly, your feet will be pretty well planted and your body balanced when you actually make your swing. However, your tendency at first will probably be to overrun the ball and find yourself too close. Nothing is more exasperating. All that effort and sprinting, and you find you have no room for a decent swing. Practice is the only cure for this habit, practice on a court or a backboard. You will gradually learn to judge distance and the amount of time it takes you to travel over it. Naturally, this applies to all shots, not just the forehand.

By now I hope you have a mental picture of how the plain, basic forehand should be hit. The main thing is to get the feeling of swinging freely. You may find that you prefer to make a round swing or a loop on your back swing before meeting the ball. This is perfectly all right as long as the racket face is flat at the moment of impact. Do what is most comfortable for you, but I would recommend starting with the simplest style first. As you improve you can afford to be more flowery.

You shouldn't spend all your time on your forehand, for you would certainly become lopsided or too fond of hitting balls on your right side.

THE BACKHAND DRIVE

Backhands always seem to frighten beginners, who treat them like the plague. It's strange that this feeling is so general because, actually, a backhand is easier to "groove" than a forehand: there is less "open racket room" on the backhand side, less danger, for the beginner, of wild flourishes. It's not really a difficult shot and, once you learn the correct way to hit it, you will be surprised to find out that you like a backhand as well as a forehand. In fact there are a few famous players who run around the center balls in order to hit them on the backhand side. Don Budge, Frankie Parker, Pauline Betz, Helen Jacobs, Darlene

Hard all favored their strong backhands this way—and not necessarily because their forehands were weak. They *preferred* the backhand.

Maybe you will too. It is important to learn from the very beginning how to hit off both wings and be prepared for a ball on either. Then you won't develop the bad habit, which grows worse with time, of running around shots. And you can visualize for yourself how it opens up too much of the court for your opponent's next shot if you move way over to run around a weakness. Make up your mind right now that hitting backhands can be fun and well worth learning.

What is the best way to hit a backhand? The first thing a beginner always has to learn is that he cannot hit a backhand with a forehand grip (unless it's the Continental forehand grip, which I mentioned earlier and didn't recommend as the best to choose). Try it with your Eastern forehand grip and you'll see that your hand is in a weak and awkward position. The grip must be changed slightly. To shift from the forehand to the backhand grip, turn the racket with the fingers of the left hand (which are supporting the shaft of the racket) for about a quarter turn to the right. This moves your right hand to the left in a position to allow you to advance the thumb diagonally upward along the handle of the back (flat) side of the racket. The thumb should not be stiff and straight up the handle: this wouldn't allow for enough mobility. But the thumb does give support and plays an important role in adding power and control to the shot.

Practice changing grips from the forehand to the backhand, and then back again to the forehand, always keeping the left hand as a bracing guide to help you to shift quickly. Do this over and over again until it begins to feel natural. Just a few seconds a day is all it takes. Then when you get on the court, you won't have to take time out to think and say to yourself, "Which way did she say to turn the racket?"

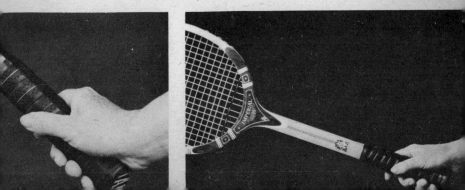

Now you are prepared for the backhand swing. Just as you did for the forehand, start from the "ready position," on the alert with your feet slightly apart, knees bent but relaxed, ready to move and turn in any direction. Your racket is in front of you resting in the palm of your left hand. You are using the forehand grip, but are ready to shift to the backhand. Here comes the ball, and it's coming to your left side— a backhand. You shift your racket to the backhand grip.

Then there are two things to do immediately and simultaneously. Take your racket back about waist high on your left side with your *two* arms, as though you were going to bat a baseball left-handed. This automatically turns your shoulders and hips sideways to the net, a position essential to freedom of movement. At the same moment take a step, with your *left* foot this time, putting your weight slightly on it, but do not anchor it. (Do as you did with your right foot for the fore-hand—remember?) Your left arm acts as a support and guide to the right arm (so that the racket head won't dip and slide), and the two work together. The elbow of the right arm stays away from the body, and the arms are comfortably extended.

You are all set to swing forward. *And you are really going to swing.* No pushing or shoving or babying of the ball! As you swing, step for-ward onto your right foot, thus transferring your weight from the left foot to the right. Try to meet the ball, as you did with the forehand, at the moment just after your weight has been transferred and about on a line with the front foot. The left arm lets go of the racket just before the ball is hit and the right arm takes over on its own. At the point of contact (as with the forehand) the face of the racket is flat against the ball and the ball is hit in the middle of the gut. Follow through as you did on the other side: again you must get the feeling that you are going to hit through the ball and almost throw the racket after it (with-out letting go). The racket will automatically finish its course up toward the right shoulder, imparting a slight top spin to the ball, which will keep it in court no matter how hard you hit it.

And that's all there is to it—*if* the ball happens to come right to you, about waist high. Of course, it seldom does.

Spin of the Ball

At this point I should tell you something about the spin of the ball

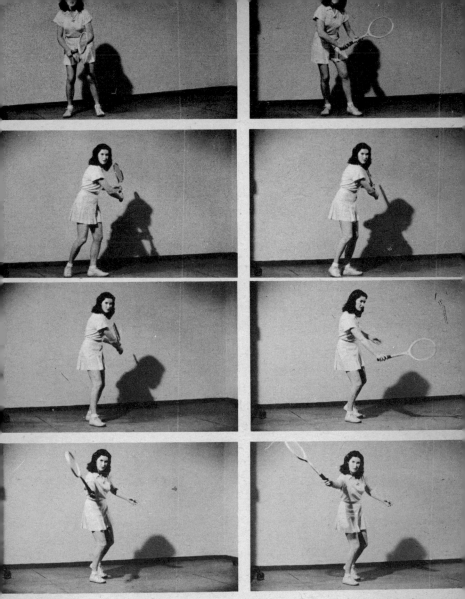

Follow the author as she hits a backhand drive. Take the racket back with both arms; turn the shoulders and hips sideways to the net; step forward onto the right foot as you begin to swing forward; transfer the weight from left to right foot; let go of the racket with the left hand; meet the imaginary ball on a line with your right foot, racket face flat against the ball; keep your balance and prepare to follow through with the racket ending up toward your right shoulder.

Bill Tilden, probably the greatest player of all time, hits an undersliced back-hand from the baseline. Notice the face of the racket slightly beveled to give the ball the desired underspin. *Edwin Levick, N.Y.*

and how you can use both top spin and slice (or underspin) for fore-hands and backhands to great advantage. The object of putting spin on the ball is twofold: the first being the control of your own stroke; the second being to discompose your opponent.

A slice is an undercut shot. The racket face is beveled back at the moment of impact, and you hit across and under the ball, thereby imparting spin. The degree of spin depends on how hard you hit the ball, how much angle you use on the head of the racket, and how long your follow-through is. Only by experimenting can you learn to put on the right amount of spin. You can learn to make the ball curve either way. A chop is made by hitting more down and under the ball, rather than across, and can be used as an attacking shot. Elizabeth Ryan had probably the most aggressive chop of any woman player I ever saw; and Bill Tilden had such control he could practically make the ball talk.

A top spin, as it implies, gives overspin to the ball. You hit it from below, with the racket face beveled forward, and swing up, thus imparting the spin that makes the ball dip down, bounce, and dart upwards.

You can understand how the use of both types of spins, if well controlled, can disrupt the timing of your opponent. However, it's better to learn the basic strokes first and experiment with the spins afterwards.

Footwork

Most of the time you will have to move, or run, for a backhand. The pattern of footwork should seem familiar to you by now. Start with the left foot, no matter in what direction (up, back, left, right, diagonal), and hold your racket back as you start to move (or trot or gallop). When you are within hitting distance of the ball, be sure that your weight is again slightly on your left foot, so that you can transfer to the right as you swing forward.

You may have wondered, while I have been discussing the forehand and the backhand, why I've omitted any discussion of the part the wrist plays in the stroking. I've avoided it on purpose, because there is nothing that befuddles a beginner so much as details about the wrist. As in golf, the wrist eventually takes care of itself. Too much concentration on wrist action in the beginning will make it artificial and exaggerated, and too much wrist can do more harm than too little.

So your shots may seem a little stiff for a while. But you will discover, as time goes on, that your wrist will automatically go to work of its own accord. For instance, at the end of the back swing the wrist bends backward or makes a slight loop before coming forward again. You will also learn that you get best results when the wrist is neither too tight nor too loose. The only time it is tightened is just before and during the actual moment of contact with the ball, when the wrist must withstand the impact. The rest of the time it is relaxed but firm.

Relaxation

Relaxation is essential always—relaxation of the mind, the body, and the swing. At times this is far from easy; you must *train* yourself to relax. This is the reason why I advise swinging the racket many, many times without the ball, so that you get the feeling of relaxing all your muscles. I must have looked rather odd to some people as I used to walk down the street swinging my racket this way and that, but why worry about such things if one is improving one's game?

Besides relaxation, there's nothing more important to your tennis than balance and rhythm. Naturally, in the beginning, you will be very "stroke-conscious"; you will be thinking too much about your technique to be aware of anything else. But as time goes on and you practice conscientiously you will find to your surprise and joy that you are having to think less and less about "how" to hit the ball. Gradually you will begin to feel that magical flow of rhythm and balance; the jerks and jolts and the pulling-up habit will slowly disappear. Your shots will become smoother, your movements more graceful and coordinated; you will be getting more power with less effort.

Balance

Balance is essential, not only during the shot, but during the follow-through. When you are making a stroke on either side with your right arm, use your left arm for balance (like a skater or skier), so that the two arms and two shoulders are synchronized. Never let the left arm hang limply by your side: let it work along with the right. And after each stroke bring your racket back to rest in your left hand to be ready for the next shot.

It is amazing what balance can do for you. There will be times when you are struggling for a shot and find yourself on the wrong foot, out of position, and it will be too late to do a darn thing about it. Just remember, when all these harrowing things happen, to keep your head, keep your balance, relax, and swing through in the direction you want the ball to go. I have seen players make a shot lying

No woman champion has been more graceful or had better balance than Maria Bueno, of São Paulo, Brazil, who was a Wimbledon winner as well as United States singles title-holder three times. Maria had to bend way down to handle this shot, which is either a mid-court low forehand or a half-volley. With her perfect balance, I'm sure the shot came off well. *World Tennis Magazine.*

flat on their backs. I have seen players get away with murder on the court: they are facing square front to the net; they are too close to the ball; they do many of the things that I have recommended that you *don't* do; yet they make the shot. But how? When they actually hit the ball they are well balanced, their timing is good and they set their weight into the shot. Consider the fabulous Jimmy Brown, the famous fullback of the Cleveland Browns; his balance is so extraordinary that he seems to be able to do things on the football field that are almost superhuman. It's mostly due to balance, say the sports writers.

I'm not suggesting that you can rely on balance alone to be a good tennis player. I'm just saying that you can do a lot of things wrong and get away with it if you do have good balance. All the same, it's better to play the sensible way—upright.

THE SERVE

There was a time long ago when the serve in lawn tennis was no more than a way of "putting the ball in play." The men served rather politely, and the ladies even served underhand. I don't blame them: in their outfits it must have been difficult to reach up. But this was in the early 1900s . . . before 1912. In that year a young man came out of the West—not Lochinvar, but Maurice McLoughlin. This young man from California was nicknamed "the Comet." It's still hard to decide which was more dazzling, his red hair or the revolutionary effect of his service on the tennis world. No one had ever seen such a serve before; nobody had used the serve as such an important attacking weapon. McLoughlin was big and powerful, and that opening shot of his came over the net with such force and spin that he either served outright aces or was able to run in to the net and put away weak returns.

Like most American boys Red McLoughlin had played baseball, football, softball and other throwing games and had developed a natural aptitude for the overhead swing. It's probably because of these games that American boys have such fine serves. In countries where rugby, soccer, and games like cricket, which involve underhand throws, are the most popular, tennis players tend to have less powerful overheads. The introduction of baseball and softball to Mexico, South America, Japan, and Puerto Rico, for instance, has greatly improved the serves of the younger tennis players in these countries. Undoubtedly girls, who learn to serve less readily than boys, ought to play more baseball. Alice Marble, Darlene Hard and Althea Gibson, whose serves were outstanding in women's tennis, all played baseball as youngsters—and not just the softball variety.

You may well ask why the Australians, who don't specialize in baseball, have such excellent serves—players like Frank Sedgman, Neale Fraser, Rod Laver, Roy Emerson, and Margaret Smith. The answer is that in Australia tennis is a major sport. It is as big a sport to them as baseball is to us. Youngsters start learning at a very early age, and, if they show unusual promise as teenagers, they are often sponsored by sporting-goods concerns (allowed by their Amateur Rules Committee—unlike ours). They can thus leave school in order to concentrate all their time and energy on tennis. Naturally their serves flourish along with the rest of their game.

Kinds of Serves

The advantages of a first-class serve must be fairly obvious to any-one who has watched good tennis. The average spectator, who may not be able to understand the intricacies of the different strokes, has no trouble recognizing and appreciating the "fast serve," sometimes known as the *cannonball*. Tennis galleries always love it. As I mentioned in the chapter "What Have You Got?," this serve is most effectively used by a very tall player, like Bill Tilden, Ellsworth Vines, Johnny Doeg, Frank Shields, Pancho Gonzalez, Frank Froehling, and many others today—all of them over 6 feet 2—who make (or made) the most of these extra inches. Elly Vines, when he was at his peak, used to hit the serve so hard that his opponent was helpless. I watched him, when he beat Bunny Austin in the finals of Wimbledon, and Henri Cochet in the U. S. National finals, make two or three service aces in a game. And Don Budge told me that on their professional tour one winter Vines averaged two service aces a game. Against a player of Budge's ability this seems nothing short of miraculous.

The *spin* serve can be remarkably devastating too. Though perhaps not so spectacular to the gallery, it is often just as annoying to an opponent—especially from a left-handed server like Johnny Doeg or

Neale Fraser. The serve comes at you looking like an egg. You hardly have time to decide which way it will jump after it lands (or which way you will have to jump).

An effective spin serve must be either fast and low or fast and high. A soft slow spin is of no use: it just sits up and says, "Hit me!" Naturally it takes great strength to hit a ball hard enough for the spin to be dangerous. This is why boys have better spin serves than girls. You can't fairly compare the serves of Gene Scott, Arthur Ashe, and Herb FitzGibbon with the serves of even the top-ranking girls; or the serve of Clark Graebner with that of his wife Carole, good though hers is.

If you're not especially strong, therefore, don't waste time with the fast, high spin, but develop the fast, low spin instead. At least your opponent won't be able to put away his return so easily—and maybe not at all.

There is a third and equally important type of service, the one which succeeds through *placement*. What others accomplish with their speed and power, you, with skill, can also achieve, through variety, deception, accuracy and surprise. It's up to you; the possibilities are unlimited.

A serve which is well placed needn't be hit tremendously hard. This should be encouraging to some of you small players, like me, who have neither the height nor the power to put great speed into the shot. Rather than get frustrated trying to do something you can't do, make up your mind that it is just as challenging (perhaps more so) to depend on brains and ingenuity. Place the serve to your opponent's weakness. If, for instance, he has a good backhand but likes to hit his forehand close to his body, you will enjoy sending a wide ball to his forehand where he will have to reach for it. If, on the other hand, he seems to like reaching for balls, serve right at him.

The Service Grip

Now for the actual hitting of the serve. Naturally we start with the grip. The grip for the service is really like the backhand grip, except that the thumb stays around the handle, instead of diagonally across it. The forefinger should be allowed to go a little way up the handle, for an added sense of touch and control.

The service grip: This grip is like the backhand grip except that the thumb curves around the handle. The forefinger is allowed to go a little way up the handle to help control the racket.

The Stance

Next comes the stance. And this is a good moment to study the foot-fault rules (Rules 6 and 7), which you will find at the back of the book. It's important for you to take a good look at them now before you develop bad habits.

My interpretation: don't walk; don't run; don't jump; don't hop. Keep both your feet *behind* the base line until your racket has hit the ball. Keep at least one foot on the ground at all times until the ball has left the racket.

Most people don't mean to foot fault: they either don't know any better or are too careless to bother about it. Yet, at all times, a foot fault is discourteous, takes an unfair advantage of your opponent, and breaks the rules. Also it's downright stupid, especially if you plan to play later in any big tournaments, where you may have a foot-fault judge. You will be the one to suffer—and needlessly. I have seen players actually lose important matches because they have become flustered when foot faults were called against them. It would have been much simpler for them to have learned the do's-and-don'ts in the beginning. The habit of swinging the back foot forward too soon over the line is a common fault; so is moving the left foot (by hopping or stepping) over the line after you think you have it planted safely behind, or taking a little jump with both feet off the ground. Habits such as these are difficult to unlearn, once you get too accustomed to the feeling. And the benefits are practically nil, unless you're a violent net-rusher and want to get a headstart of a few feet towards the net—a totally unsportsmanlike tactic.

Enough for foot faults—just avoid making them.

Position for Service

Besides making sure that you are legally behind the base line (5 or 6 inches should be safe, even if your left toe swerves a bit forward), it is equally important for you to serve from the most advantageous position you are allowed. You may have noticed that most of the leading players, when serving from the right side in singles, stand near the center of the court (it's a foot fault if you go to the left of center, though). They do this for two reasons: one is to be in a position to protect any part of their court when the service is returned; the other is to have a more direct aim at the opponent's backhand. You'll be wise to follow their example. This doesn't mean that you shouldn't vary your position from time to time, especially if you have a good sizzling slice serve that could curve into the opponent if you were to stand farther to the right, or that could curve out of his reach if you were to stand way to the right and serve wide to the forehand. But you would be exposing more areas of unprotected court. Your serve had better be exceptionally good if you take this risk.

Now for the actual stance. Place your feet comfortably apart, with the left foot in front and the right foot behind, and your body turned slightly sideways to the net. If, for instance, you were to draw an imaginary line between your two feet, this line should point in the direction of the court you are serving into. You should be almost evenly balanced as you start to swing.

Hold the balls in your left hand. I can hold only two comfortably, but some people like to hold three, in case of a let ball. The current vogue among many of our ranking men players is to hold only one in the left hand and stash an extra ball or two in the left pocket of their shorts. You may choose for yourself. Rest the head or throat of your racket on or across your left hand and have the racket head point toward the service court to give yourself a last-minute aim in the right direction.

The swing is very much like the throw of a baseball, without the preliminary windup—except, of course, that you have a racket in your hand instead of a ball. Practice swinging a few times without actually tossing up the ball with your left arm (just pretend to throw it up) until you begin to feel that the swing is natural. Swing the racket smoothly down and back and up to shoulder height. The elbow will automatically bend as you start swinging up and forward to meet the ball at the peak of the arc, with your right arm extended. Follow through straight out in front of you, almost as though you were going to throw the racket out after the ball, before the racket continues its course across the body and ends down toward your left side. Your weight shifts forward as you swing up and forward, stretching to meet the ball at the highest possible point in order to get the benefit of every inch of reach.

The Toss

The most difficult part of the serve, as any beginner soon discovers, is to coordinate the swing with the toss, so that racket and ball meet at the right place at the right time. Only practice will develop good timing and produce this minor miracle. At first you will probably have trouble learning a good toss (most people do), let alone making it synchronize with the swing. Remember you never need hit a bad toss in a game: let the ball drop and have another try. I've even seen tournament players do this in the middle of a match. Louise Brough did it quite often. It's perfectly acceptable, especially when there's a strong wind blowing.

The best way to decide where the ball should be thrown is to start a practice swing without the ball, and then *halt* at its peak. When you stop the racket try to memorize exactly the spot above you where the middle of the gut is. This is the spot you must aim for in your toss, or a fraction above, because you ought to hit the ball near the top of the throw or just barely after it starts to drop. Practice throw-

Jack Kramer, former United States and Wimbledon Champion. Notice Jack's shoulders and hips sideways ready to uncoil and reach up for the ball at the height of the toss. *Press Association, Inc.*

ing the ball up with the left hand alone, without the right-arm swing, to the spot you have chosen. Let your fingers seem to guide the ball, with your arm following up after it. Never be afraid to throw the ball high enough: better too high than too low. You need plenty of time to make a full swing. And be sure to throw far enough in front so that your weight will be coming forward into the shot and enough to the right to enable you to swing clear of your body without bashing yourself on the knee.

What I have just described is a plain serve, without spins or twists of any kind. At the moment of impact the racket face is flat against the ball. This is the one to learn first. After some practice with the plain serve you will be ready to experiment with the two service variations, the slice and the American twist.

The Slice

To serve a slice, throw the ball a little farther to the *right* than you normally would and hit across it and down from right to left (the farther to the right you throw it, the sharper the slice). The spin imparted to the ball keeps it low, makes it bounce close to the ground and to your opponent's right side. This serve can be very useful on slow or wet courts or against a slow player who doesn't like to bend or be drawn out of court. It's most effective when used for change of pace, either before or after a fast serve. It can also be a safe second serve or a surprise first serve. Naturally, the harder you hit the ball, the better the spin.

The American Twist

For the American, or reverse, twist—the one that bounces from left to right—throw the ball farther to the *left* than usual and back over your head. (But don't try this if you don't have a strong back.) Hit up and out at the ball, this time with the racket swinging from left to right and following through away from your body on the right side. The spin you give to the ball will cause it to bounce to your opponent's left side. As with the slice, the harder you hit, the better the spin. You can see how this serve will be especially useful against a person with a weak backhand. But in order to give the ball enough spin to produce a high-kicking bounce and to make the serve really effective, you must arch your back and really whack the ball, with

Champion Althea Gibson, in 1957, serves an American twist. Notice how she gets her body well around and reaches up to get full benefit of her height.

a strong snap of the wrist. This motion, as you will see if you try, often proves too tiring for the average girl. And it's not worth the extra effort to a boy, either, unless he's unusually strong.

Many players use the American twist as a reliable second serve in singles, especially on a court with a fast surface, like asphalt or cement, because the high bounce forces an opponent back. It's valuable in doubles too, as either a first or second serve, because it also allows the server extra time to run in to the net himself.

The serve is the player's choice. The average player uses the plain serve for a first serve and the "safe" slice for the second. The more ambitious player, who wants as much variety as possible, uses all three serves. To achieve a really fine serve involves practice—no part of the game takes as much hard work as the serve. On the other hand it has one great advantage: it's the only stroke you can practice by yourself. All you need is a basket of used balls (they don't even have to bounce) and a court with a net. Serve your basketful across the net, walk over, pick them up, and serve them back. There's no limit to the amount of skill you can acquire, if you have the necessary patience and endurance.

One word of caution, though. Don't be so overenthusiastic in the beginning that you get a sore arm. Treat your arm with the respect a pitcher shows his: warm up gradually—and don't overdo.

THE VOLLEY

Volleying, to me, is really the most exciting part of tennis. When you try it, you'll see why. If I sound slightly prejudiced, I probably am, since volleying is the best part of my game. The whole situation is exhilarating: you have made your forcing shot: you're up at the net; your opponent is on the run—and you are ready for the kill! Then you make the volley, sudden and dramatic. I don't believe you can help from getting a feeling of satisfaction when you finish off a point this way.

Of course things don't always work out according to your plan. Perhaps your forcing shot turns out to be a dud, and the tables are turned. There you are at the net (it's too late to turn back) and the best you can manage is a desperation return. But don't dwell on your failures—there's always another chance.

Today the volley is an essential part of your tennis repertory, whether you want to win or just have fun. Rallies in the best boys' matches nearly always end at the net; and this is more and more true of girls' matches too. Maureen Connolly, for instance, who had such great ground strokes, finally realized how important the volley was. Before her unfortunate horseback-riding accident, which ended her tournament career, she was improving her volleying month by month, even though it didn't come naturally to her. I believe if Nancy Richey followed her example, she'd have a better chance of beating Champion Margaret Smith. Of course one must have the temperament to make the volleying really effective, but that can be developed to a certain extent. There are some people, due to poor eyesight, or very slow reflexes, or a strong fear of bodily harm, who shouldn't volley. For the rest of you though, who have average ability plus the spirit of fun and adventure, volleying is practically a must. (Not at the expense of your ground strokes, please!)

Gone are the days of the long endless rallies from the back court, which were really as much a test of patience and endurance as of good stroking. I remember reading once of a famous match which took place on the Riviera, years ago, between Mrs. Satterthwaite of England and Lucy Valerio of Italy. They made tennis history then; but what happened would be impossible today. Apparently these two ladies had such a long rally that some spectators got bored and went to have tea, only to discover upon their return that the same rally was still in progress. Over two hundred shots had been hit. Two men playing a match on the next court had completed an entire set.

Obviously this couldn't happen today. Any modern player would certainly be able to force a weak or short return eventually, which he could follow to the net for the winning volley.

It was Mrs. Wightman who, as Hazel Hotchkiss from California, in 1909 first popularized the volley in girls' tennis and showed what could be accomplished up at the net. Her amazing anticipation, quick reflexes, and clever placing of the ball enabled her to volley back the hardest balls in the most uncanny way. She could hold her own in volleying exchanges even against the good male players. It was she who taught me to love volleying. We had a great time trying to outwit each other when we were opponents—and we worked like clockwork when we played as a team. In fact we won the National Indoor Women's Doubles together, when I was only fifteen, playing against far more powerful hitters.

Now for the volleying stroke itself. The hitter is usually up at the net—that is, between the net and the service line. The player's exact position, or the closeness to the net, depends entirely on his height and reach. Ideally speaking, you would like to be two or three feet back of the net since, the nearer you are to it, the easier it is for you to hit down on the ball with real vigor. Realistically, however, you must be able to cover all possible lobs. So unless you're very tall, quick, and have a long reach, you'll have to settle for standing farther back. Only trial and error will determine your own best position.

The Volley Grip

The volley is not a full stroke. You need hardly any back swing for a volley, and the faster the ball comes to you the less back swing is necessary. For a very fast ball, hold your wrist firm to withstand the shock of impact and almost block the ball, using your opponent's speed to send it back over the net. For a slower ball you may use slight back swing because you must provide your own power and give the ball a real punch. The higher the ball, the harder you can punch it with comparative safety.

Thinking that the volley is a full stroke is the error most beginners fall into. They take the racket back as for a full swing, and by that time the ball has already gone by. The volley is a *punch*, a solid punch of a ball that is well in front of you. Try to go forward to meet it. The grip for the forehand volley may be either the service grip or the forehand grip. I prefer the service grip because it involves less changing for the backhand, and one has so little time in a rapid-fire exchange. It's possible, if you get caught, to hit a backhand volley with the service grip. You'd be in a dilemma if you had to face a backhand volley with your Eastern forehand grip. The best backhand volley grip is the same as for the backhand drive, with the thumb diagonally up the handle, providing extra power and punch to your shot. For either the forehand or backhand volley, holding the racket an inch or so farther up the shaft than usual will give you extra control. This is especially true for younger players, or those without a strong right wrist and arm.

Hitting the Volley

While hitting the volley keep the racket head *above* your wrist. This is very important. Then hit down and across the ball as you would if you were chopping at an object. In other words, the punch isn't perfectly flat—it has a slight undercut to it. This keeps the ball from flying over the base line or into the net and, while giving you a much greater margin of safety, still allows you to hit as hard as you want. Watch Bill Talbert and Gardnar Mulloy sometime, if you get a chance, to see how they hit their volleys—excellent models to emulate.

You can understand why the high volley is much easier to hit down and across than the low volley. When the ball is low, you must bend your knees way down in a crouching position, so that when you hit the ball the racket head will still be *above the wrist*. In this way you can still cut (or chop) the low balls and aim them just over the net.

You will often find during rapid exchanges at the net that you haven't time to turn your feet around sideways to the net (as you should and can do with your ground strokes). Try at least to pivot your shoulders slightly for added power.

The forehand volley: Keep the racket head *above* the wrist. You need hardly any backswing for a volley. Hold your wrist firm and *punch* away and across the ball well in front of you. The face of the racket is slightly beveled back.

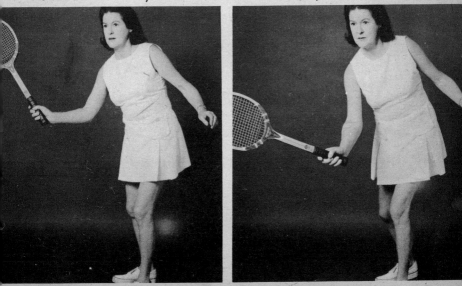

Another fine champion and sportsman, Roy Emerson of Australia, winner of both United States and Wimbledon Championships, is shown here hitting a difficult high backhand volley to Raphael Osuna, the brilliant Mexican player, who won our championship in 1963. *Australian News and Information Bureau Photograph.*

The most important rule of volleying is to keep your eyes, mind and feet on the alert all the time. Then you will be able to get ready in time to hit the ball in front of your body. Gradually your reflexes will speed up automatically and you will loose your timidity. It is when people are surprised or caught napping that they feel rushed and become flustered.

As you will soon discover, there are right and wrong times to run in to the net, and there are good and bad ways to do it. Only by practicing can you figure out what is best for you. This is especially true in singles, where you have no partner to share the court and your problems with you. Your serve must be especially strong if you are to follow it in consistently with any hope of success.

The Great Volleyers

There have been many great volleyers in tennis history. Some are famous for a powerful high forehand volley or a wicked backhand slice volley; some for a delicate drop volley, or a low forehand barely-over-the-top-of-the-net volley, or a half volley (sometimes known as a pickup). Two of the greatest men volleyers I ever saw were Vinnie Richards and George Lott. Vinnie could hit a volley from any height in any direction, with extraordinary consistency, deception and pace. George could too, but he relied a little more on touch and finesse, such as interrupting a fast exchange with a subtle lob volley. Both could handle any speed and put away an overhead smash despite their lack of height.

Among the women, besides Mrs. Wightman, one of the all-time great volleyers, Alice Marble volleyed as well as any I have seen or played with: she did it remarkably like a boy, being both quick and powerful. Like Maria Bueno, Alice used considerable wrist motion and was therefore more brilliant on some days than others, the way Maria is. A shot made with a flexible wrist calls for fine timing. Though not consistently accurate, this type of volley at its best is sensational.

Margaret Osborne Dupont was, and still is, a great volleyer. She is another player who can hit any kind of a shot, shoulder high, waist high, ankle low, or sky high, off both wings (forehand or backhand) with equal effectiveness. Although Margaret, in her championship days, lacked the agility of Alice and Maria, she made up for it through her great anticipation and accuracy.

Still another of the volleying greats was Darlene Hard. Considering her stocky build, it was amazing how fast she could cover the court at her peak in 1960 and 1961. Here again was a player who had the quick reflexes and power of a boy yet delicacy with a touch volley when needed. Her backhand volley was a joy to watch. Though she had a fine sense of anticipation, she would occasionally crowd the net too closely and be vulnerable to a surprise lob over her head.

Margaret Osborne Dupont, former United States and Wimbledon champion in singles and doubles, is shown here hitting a low volley.

There is one thing that all these superior volleyers had in common: *they loved being up at the net.* You too can learn to like it if you have the spirit to try. But don't be foolhardy and run in on any old shot, just because you liked the way Lew Hoad or Rod Laver did it. Keep within your own limitations and discover as you play which are the right and wrong times to run in. Above all, learn sound ground strokes and a good serve so that you'll have the right shots to follow up to the net, when the occasion arises, with a reasonable chance of success. Only then will you realize the great thrill to be derived from volleying well.

THE HALF VOLLEY (OR PICKUP)

There is another stroke you should know about, one that may come in very handy at times—the half volley. It may be used defensively or aggressively, depending on the circumstances. Actually I think it is confusingly named, since it is more like a half ground stroke than a volley. Because it is a shot hit a split second after it has bounced, it takes split-second timing to hit it correctly. You will often use a half volley when you get caught halfway in on your way to make a volley, because either you have chosen the wrong shot or have misjudged the distance, and the ball dips towards your feet. Obviously you don't have time to make a full stroke of it. What to do? First—don't panic. Next, take your racket back as you would for a low ground stroke, but not so far back. With this short back swing, and with your knees well bent, you hit the ball just after it hits the ground. You don't need much follow-through: you pick up your speed from the momentum of the rising ball.

Getting the correct level of the racket face is the trickiest part. It takes a sensitive touch and accurate timing. To return the ball low (which you ordinarily should), turn the racket face slightly downward to offset the rising ball; if you want to aim the ball higher for some tactical reason, level the face farther back. Experiment a few times to get the feel. The half volley is definitely a "touch" shot.

The half volley used defensively can extricate you from a predicament, as we have seen. It can also be used successfully as an aggressive weapon, if you have unusually good timing and are exceptionally quick. Henri Cochet (France), Dick Williams (USA), and Fred Perry (England) were all great players of some years ago. I saw each of these

(Left) The half volley: The backswing is short, the knees well bent as you hit the ball on the rise just as it bounces. The racket face is beveled slightly forward. *(Right)* One of the great volleyers and tennis artists of all times is the Australian Ken Rosewall, now a leading professional player. He's in a beautiful position to hit a low backhand volley. Notice his perfect poise and balance.

players at his prime handle a ball on the rise in an amazingly aggressive fashion, as either a forceful running-in shot or an offensive passing shot. A few of the top American and Australian players can do this today, although not so consistently. It's a risky thing to do, since, as I said, it takes such perfect timing, and your chances of mistiming are considerable. Use it therefore when you feel "right," as a surprise maneuver to harry your opponent, or for the sheer fun of it. If you happen to connect just right it will feel like magic and you'll wonder if you were the one who actually made the shot.

THE LOB

You may be one of the many who think (erroneously) that a lob is only a high defensive shot that you hit when you're in trouble in order to give yourself time to catch your breath and get back into position. It's a good time to realize now that the lob can be also one of the most deadly and unpleasant surprises in tennis. So it's worth learning a good one. Surprise and disguise are important elements in its success. If well timed and solidly hit, it catches an opponent off guard, therefore off balance. If it's not hit too high, it doesn't give him much time to scurry back and retrieve it.

Hitting the Lob

To hit a lob, take your racket back as you would for a regular ground stroke. This time, though, meet the ball with the face of your racket leveled back (rather than flat) and follow through upward instead of straight forward. No pushing or shoving: hit it firmly. Remember not to jerk or pull your body up—the stroke should be both smooth and solid, as in a trap shot in golf, when the club will do the lifting, not your arms or body.

Placement

A lob must be well placed: its success depends on your opponent—on his height, his reach, his ability to run back, and of course his overhead smash. Try to figure out what kind of lob gives him the most trouble. Perhaps he takes a full swing and likes the high ones but can't adjust to a lower ball. Perhaps he likes them low but has trouble with the high soft floaters which fall down on him. The arrows of William the Conqueror's men had a devastating effect on King Harold and his followers at Hastings. Lobs, like arrows, can change the whole tide of battle.

Besides deciding these things for yourself, there are problems of execution for you to solve: you must learn to judge the arc, or the course, the lob will take as you estimate how deep and how hard you can hit the ball without sending it over the base line. If your opponent

The Lob: The backswing is like that for a ground stroke. Meet the ball firmly with the face of the racket leveled back and follow through upward.

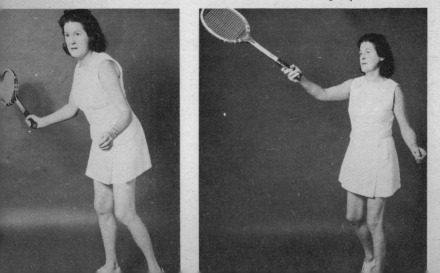

is standing as far back as the service line, you will find it difficult to hit one over his head that will also stay in court. The best time to lob is when he is in very close to the net.

I shall never forget the finals of the Women's Nationals in 1958 when Althea Gibson was playing Darlene Hard. Althea, the defending champion, was the odds-on favorite; but Darlene was having one of her dauntless, daring days. To most everyone's surprise she won the first set 6-3 and seemed on her way to causing a big upset. Everything was going right for her—her service, her return of serve, her volleying and overhead. Naturally her spirits were in high gear as she rushed confidently up to the net . . . too close as it turned out. Rather than getting flustered, Althea took stock of the situation and decided to do something about it. At the beginning of the second set "it happened." Within the space of the first two games Althea made three perfect lobs over Darlene's head as she was zooming in, all landing within an inch or two of the base line. Darlene's serve was broken (and with it her morale); the whole complexion of the match changed. Her confidence shaken, Darlene no longer dared to rush so close to the net. Althea began to take the offensive and won the last two sets 6-1, 6-2.

Here's a piece of advice about the lob that's decidedly worth remembering: it's safe to say that no one (except perhaps Don Budge) particularly relishes a surprise lob over his backhand side. There are two reasons for this. In the first place very few people have the strength to put away a high backhand for a winner. It's a tough shot. To place it—easy enough; but to put away—very difficult. Secondly, it's awkward to run around this shot to put it away on your forehand side, especially if you haven't much time.

Another good use for the lob is a surprise top-spin lob (not for beginners, obviously). Instead of leveling the face of the racket back at the moment of impact, you level it slightly forward but still follow through way up, thus imparting lots of top spin to the ball. The result is a shot that looks as though it's going yards over the base line, but the top spin takes hold and brings the ball down well within bounds.

Bobby Riggs, an expert lobber, was one of the great proponents of this top-spin lob. He seemed to have a perfect sense of when and where to lob; when to slow down or push back a net rusher; when to change the pace of the game; and when to give himself time to recover his position. In other words he knew how to use the lob both defensively and offensively, much to the agony of his opponents. As for his accuracy—again and again I heard his opponents mutter, "That lucky stiff!," as one of Bobby's lobs floated by overhead and landed on a line. Points won this way often may be disheartening, but, believe me, they are not all due to luck.

Lobbing is an art which you should cultivate. It pays rich dividends and will help you to win matches.

THE OVERHEAD SMASH

Spectators often groan when a player knocks a seemingly easy smash out of court, as if to say, "How could he make such a stupid error?" They love to watch a powerful overhead and shriek when a ball is bounced over the backstop or into the grandstand (as I've seen Bob Falkenburg and Cliff Drysdale do in the Forest Hills Stadium —no easy feat). Some players thrive on the all-powerful feeling it gives them to "murder" the ball, whether in front of a gallery or not. But they are not the wise ones: they're the very ones who are apt to miss the setups and most important shots.

Now what happens when your opponent lobs to you? You know it's not easy to smash the ball away. Placement and less speed will serve your purpose just as well if not better. In the long run the really fine overhead is the one that is accurate and consistent: you must learn to smash either deep or short, straight or angled. There's plenty to concentrate on without taking unnecessary chances, so don't distract yourself by summoning every last ounce of strength and shooting for the dramatic. Be content to settle for a well-placed winner. Naturally, if there's an easy opening, you shoot hard and fast.

The overhead smash is hit very much like the serve, but without a completely full swing. The grip is the same as for the serve. The difficulty is in timing and judgment: you must estimate the flight of the lob so that you can be there to hit the ball at the same spot in the air as you would a serve. When the falling lob reaches this point, meet the ball and smash it—in the middle of the gut.

(Left) Arthur Ashe, the outstanding star from Richmond, Virginia, and, in 1965, the first Negro player to be elected a member of the United States Davis Cup team, is preparing to hit an overhead smash. Since then Arthur has become a top-ranking professional, having won the first U.S. Open title in 1968. Now he has joined the W.C.T. group and is making good money. *(Right)* Champion of the 1930's Ellsworth Vines from California is about to lay into an overhead smash. He appears to be really enjoying it.

Approaching the Smash

How to get into position to accomplish this miraculous juncture that seems as difficult as the meeting of space capsules in space? As soon as you see a lob is coming, get your shoulders around sideways to the net *immediately* and take your racket back and up to shoulder height; then start moving your feet. Be sure, as you do this, that your knees are flexible and springy. The footwork for the smash is apt to be difficult for beginners: it's hard at first to manipulate your feet backward. You will find that moving *diagonally* backward on either side is much easier than trying to go straight back. For best results you will learn to use a "running-diagonal" or "slide-and-skip" step, keeping your body sideways as you go. Occasionally, for a very deep lob, when you really have to hurry, you may turn around and run, with your back to the net. But it takes quick judgment to get well behind the ball in time to turn sideways again and hit it on the bounce. If you don't judge it accurately you may find yourself too far away from the ball or too close to it.

Here is the 1965 Wimbledon and United States champion, Margaret Smith Court of Australia, practicing in Melbourne. She has just hit one of her deadly overhead smashes.

Margaret became winner of the grand slam in 1970, holder of the Australian, French, British at Wimbledon and the United States Championships in one year, the only girl besides Maureen Connolly to have done so.

It's particularly important in smashing to use a continuous rhythmical swing: swing forward as if you were serving. The elbow and wrist bend naturally (as with the throw of a ball), and you swing up and forward and down. Hit the ball in front of you if you can. A very short lob can be hit quite a bit in front; your swing will be directed more sharply downward. When the lob is a deep one, be sure that you hit well *out* and through before the racket swings down for the follow-through.

Another vital fact to remember is to give the ball a good solid blow. If it's a mistake to hit the ball harder than you should, it's just as wrong to be overcautious, since the main purpose of this stroke is to put the ball away. Try to effect the right compromise for yourself alone, not too hard, not too soft, but within your own capabilities. Then the shot will be consistently either so well placed or so strongly hit that it will seldom come back.

6 · COMPETITION? NO, THANKS

There are some people who, no matter how much they're coaxed, needled or even bribed, simply cannot stand the strain or the idea of competing against others in any field of endeavor. Something inside them rebels at the thought—in fact makes them physically ill. Possibly half of these people can change, or be changed, over the years, either by gradual participation and the subsequent gain of confidence; or by expert guidance from an understanding person (preferably not a parent) who can help them realize the satisfaction of trying to do something better than somebody else.

If, however, you are one of those who don't give a hoot about excelling, or even bettering the other guy; who only wants the pleasure of doing a thing for the sake of the thing itself (whether it be paddling a canoe, knitting a sweater or painting a picture), you must not feel inferior and think that there's something odd about you. Don't worry. You have lots of company. Decide right now that you are one of those noncompetitive people, and, by golly, you're not going to let it bother you. Go right on enjoying yourself.

Just one request, please. Before you decide once and for all that you are anticombative, be sure you have at least given yourself an honest chance to find out by experimenting. Try a few easy matches, for example, where the results don't matter. In other words, don't give up before you start, and don't form definite conclusions about yourself so quickly that you may regret it later.

Perhaps, also, you're being swayed by your parents, without even being aware of it. I have seen this happen many times. A well-meaning but overly ambitious parent can play a big part in causing a would-be player to turn against competition. Parents often want so much for their sons and daughters to succeed that they bring about the very opposite result by pushing too hard. Usually this starts when the parents—or one of them—are good tennis players themselves. They are so interested in the game that they want you, their offspring, to get the same enjoyment out of it that they do. What they don't realize is that, for this same reason, you will shy away: you will feel that in a sense you are competing with your parents, because you don't think you will ever be anywhere near as good as they. If you can understand *why* you don't want to try, you will discover that you *can* have the same fun out of tennis, without feeling that you're competing with them.

But how? My suggestion would be to start playing casually on your own, without telling your parents the details of how often or with whom. In this way you can find out for yourself what you think of tennis. If you happen to be good, that's great. Get started; get interested and continue. But don't be too eager to tell them about it—yet—or they'll want to get into the act. At this point you won't know whether or not you want to compete at all. Unless you're sure you do (in which case you'll thank your lucky stars for a competitive parent), you'll be wise not to be too communicative.

This method may sound sneaky, but it really isn't. It's just helping you find out about your own ability and interest in tennis, without interference.

If, after all this self-analysis, you have firmly made up your mind that competition is not for you, there is no rule that says you can't change it some day. *And you can still have a wonderful time playing tennis!* Unlike your sweaty, competitive friends, you can stay calm, cool and poised. You can give much more attention to your appearance because it's not so likely to suffer. What fun if you're a girl! As you have most likely noticed in newspaper and magazine ads nowadays, there are some very attractive tennis dresses and outfits on the market that can bring out your best features and show you at your most glamorous. Pamper yourself (within your budget)! Beauty and fashions are for you.

No such luck in my day: tennis fashions were practically nonexistent. During the 1930s the tennis dresses and shorts were comfortable and functional, but certainly not flattering to the figure. And we players usually had to have them custom-made at considerable expense. They took hours to dry, too (not like your drip-dries of today), especially in humid weather. In fact (aside from our tennis strokes), laundry was our number-one problem. You can imagine the size of a champion's tennis wardrobe. How well I remember Helen Wills with her pleated skirts (she always preferred a two-piece outfit). They were made of cotton and were always immaculate and perfectly ironed. She seemed to have an endless supply. I never understood how she managed it.

Then came the era of "tennis shorts," with Helen Jacobs leading the list of those who dared wear them on the famed Centre Court at Wimbledon. Her shorts were beautifully tailored, to be sure, but hardly feminine looking. Some of us, like Kay Stammers and myself, tried to combine the femininity of a skirt with the comfort of shorts, by wearing divided, pleated shorts (at a discreet, not-too-short length of course). Next came Alice Marble with her "short shorts" and nifty legs. This caused considerable comment (almost 100-per-cent favorable).

After the war, when materials were still scarce, it was some time before tennis fashions came into their own. It took a talented, imaginative English designer, named Teddy Tinling, plus an unusually attractive American tennis player, named Gertrude Moran, to bring tennis fashions to the forefront in the public eye. In fact, "Gorgeous Gussie" Moran became better known than the reigning Wimbledon champion after appearing in her famous lace panties on the Centre Court—and not just in the sports pages but in most newspaper columns, including the political ones, believe it or not.

Since that moment, tennis apparel has become almost as important a part of a girl's tennis life as her capabilities. You need not be a winner to be the focus of admiring attention on a tennis court.

For you noncompetitive young men though, the case is quite different. No one makes fun of a girl missing many shots if she looks pretty doing it. You'd do better to look casual if you can't back up a natty appearance with a good game. For some reason there is something slightly ridiculous about a boy who appears on the court attired in a new white shirt, well-cut shorts, a clean Davis Cup sweater, white socks and sneakers . . . and then can't even hit a serve in court.

Far better if you appear in something nonpretentious . . . not dirty, but obviously worn, as though you hadn't had time to go home and change but had just dropped by, hoping to get a game, since you were slightly out of practice. Now when you miss your forehands and serves (even though the form looks good), everyone will

The author at the age of about twelve. Yes—those are bloomers and white cotton stockings rolled down.

A fashion show sponsored by Kodel, and staged at Forest Hills before the matches in 1965. Mrs. Wightman (third from right) was the guest of honor, and she wore a reproduction of the kind of dress that her mother sewed for her by hand in the early 1900s. The beautiful brunette, front right, is Mrs. Dolly Seixas (Vic's wife).

say it's too bad you don't play more often—you could be so good if you only had a chance to practice. Every shot you hit well will be a sign of what you *could* do . . . if only. . . .

Good Form a Goal

As for the strokes themselves—and this applies to noncompetitives of either sex—here is where you can really enjoy yourselves by learning how to hit the ball well and smoothly. The pleasure of good stroke production can and should be a goal. Don't worry about absolute accuracy. Since you're not anxious about winning the points or games, you can spend more time on good form. There is a real thrill in meeting a ball squarely in the middle of your racket (on the gut, that is) with your weight at the right place at the right time at point of contact. Almost magically, with no feeling of effort on your part, the ball just zooms off exactly where you intended. The resulting sensation is worth hours of practice. Naturally there will be more times than not when this doesn't happen, and you'll find yourself lunging and jerking and spending a great deal of effort with minimal results. However, the few satisfactory ones will more than make up for the bad, and, as time goes on, the percentage will level off.

Try, if possible, to find someone to rally with who is better than you (a pro, if possible), who can get the ball back over and over again.

Two attractive yet comfortable tennis dresses that will keep you calm, cool and poised. You don't have to be an expert to be popular.

First practice hitting cross-court forehands; then cross-court back-hands; then down-the-line forehands and down-the-line backhands. Next practice serving from both sides of the court, first to the fore-hand side and then to the backhand side.

And by all means get up to the net and practice volleying and hitting overheads.

The volleying will come more naturally (and therefore be more en-joyable) to you boys, since nature gave the average boy quicker re-flexes and stronger wrists than most girls. Not that there can't be exceptions: Alice Marble and Darlene Hard had almost as quick reflexes as the best men players. The average girl, however, has to learn to like volleying (like eating olives and oysters), because, being slightly timid and self-protective, she'll be afraid of being hit in the stomach or face by the ball. She probably will do the worst thing pos-sible, which is to back up and shy away. The correct philosophy, when you're up at the net, should be, "I hope the next shot comes in my direction so I can get a crack at it!," instead of, "Oh-oh, I hope the next shot goes to my partner rather than to me." The only way to be *positive* about volleying is to practice enough volleys that you lose your fear. Only then will you begin to enjoy playing net. Believe me,

Dick Savitt, former Wimbledon Champion, and three-time winner of the United States Indoor National Singles, is shown here hitting a low deep forehand drive. Dick's ground strokes off both wings have always been rated among the best.

it's well worth the effort, because volleying exchanges are one of the great joys of tennis.

So are overhead smashes. Ask your obliging opponent to send up some lobs so that you can practice going back correctly (explained in the chapter on basic strokes). Also ask him to serve to you, so you cultivate a reliable return of service: first get him to serve to your forehand; then to your backhand, from both sides. He won't mind doing this, since he'll be getting such good service practice. Then offer to do the same for him to help him improve his return of serve.

If you work at all these shots enough times it won't seem like work at all. You'll be surprised how much you'll improve. On a goodwill tour of South America in 1942, when Jack Kramer was one of our country's top players (but not yet champion), he would often ask me to go out on a court with him in Buenos Aires in the mornings. He would do this even when we had matches in the afternoons, and just hit backhands, backhands, backhands . . . to improve his own backhand which he felt wasn't as good as it could be. It didn't take him long to overcome any weakness he might have had on his left wing. Me, too . . . and it surely didn't seem like drudgery.

When I was twelve years old and having trouble with my forehand (a terribly worrisome situation to me at the time), Bill Tilden, who was the world champion, took the interest and the time (also in the middle of a tournament) to meet me on the court a couple of mornings at the Longwood Cricket Club just to exchange forehand drives and to help iron out the kinks in mine.

Hitting one stroke over and over may sound boring; but it's really exhilarating when you do it on the court and discover yourself improving. Unlike when you practice scales on the piano, your whole body is in active, stimulating motion. The better you get, the better you'll want to be. Perhaps, after batting the ball around on sunny days, you will enjoy it so much that you won't hesitate to enter resort round-robin tournaments (see information on round-robin matches in Chapter 11), which is a good way to meet people; and you won't even mind being last on a school or club tennis ladder. And who knows . . . maybe the time will come when you'll want to win a match in spite of yourself.

7 · COMPETITION? YES, PLEASE

I know you. You are the eager-beaver type. You didn't choose to be: you were born that way. No matter what you tackle, you want to do it better than the other fellow. You'll practically knock yourself out just to get into the thick of battle. You are probably accused of being more stubborn than you really are, because you don't concede easily or admit defeat until the last dying gasp. Then if you're beaten, you bounce right back and are ready to start all over again, no matter what your field of endeavor. You simply thrive on the excitement of competition. Tennis is the ideal game for you. It is for me—I am one of you. It will do a lot to bring out your best qualities (like using your head and heart), and control some of your worst (like impatience, a bad temper and unharnessed nervous energy).

As I mentioned earlier, the sooner you begin tennis the better. This applies especially to you competitive players. In California, for instance, where they have so many up-and-coming young players and

(Left) A real competitor, Cliff Richey, of San Angelo, Texas, hits a shoulder-high backhand drive. Cliff was National Junior Champion in 1963. As an independent pro he was ranked No. 1 in the men's division in 1970 and is one of our best professionals. *World Tennis Magazine. (Right)* Two National Champions in one family! The father, Julius D. Heldman, is giving a few hints to his daughter, Julie M., about her forehand grip. The instruction probably isn't necessary, for young Julie has one of the best forehands in the game.

year-round tennis, if a youngster isn't winning junior tournaments by the age of fourteen, he isn't considered to have much of a future, or a chance of becoming any sort of a champ in big-league tennis. I'm not insinuating that you necessarily want to become the number-one player in the country, but you probably would like to be able to make your school, and later your college, team, as well as win some local club or state titles, at least.

My brother John knew that he couldn't spend the amount of time that his sisters did chasing around to different tournaments. He was more involved in serious studies, aiming for a future law career. Yet he was competitive and loved tennis. He became good enough to win a couple of Massachusetts State Junior Doubles titles and to make the Harvard tennis team, which offered him the great opportunity of being sent to England, along with the Yale team, to compete against the combined Oxford and Cambridge team.

There are many fine college graduates, like Gene Scott and Herb FitzGibbon, both ranked nationally, who don't necessarily want to make tennis their entire lives, but who have had marvelous trips to many parts of the world because they excel at tennis. This is likewise

One of the author's proudest moments—election to the National Lawn Tennis Hall of Fame at Newport, Rhode Island, in 1963, along with her fellow "enshrinees," Johnny Van Ryn (far right) and Julian S. Myrick (second from right). (Wilmer Allison was unable to attend in person.) Here we are receiving our citations from James H. Van Alen, the president of the Lawn Tennis Hall of Fame and originator of the new scoring system, VASSS.

true of the girls: Billie Jean Moffitt King, Nancy Richey and Carole
Graebner, to name a few, have traveled widely—because of tennis.
All of them attended college, and they all made the U.S. Wightman
Cup Team, the goal of competitive girls, as is the Davis Cup Team
for the competitive boys. In 1965 all the first ten girls had attended
or were attending college.

Since you like to compete, you're starting with a big advantage.
You can first strive to make a Junior Davis Cup or Wightman Cup
team and advance from there. The first step is to learn how to use
your head to win points, games, sets and matches. As I discussed in
the chapter "What Have You Got?," there is a way of figuring what
kind of game is best suited to your physical and mental makeup. But
now I'm going to show you how you can win just by choosing the
right style.

Choosing the Right Style

If you have watched any tournament matches lately at a club or on
television, you must have noticed that there are two distinctly different styles of play: the offensive and the defensive. One player may be
hitting with great power, while the other fellow is running all over
creation, sending up lobs and retrieving shots as best he can. Usually
the player with the power is a big, tall person, like Pancho Gonzalez
or Margaret Smith. The rushing retriever is most likely comparatively
small, like Bobby Riggs or Raphael Osuna.

As first glance you will assume that the power hitter has to be the
winner. But on closer observation you will find that very often the
fellow who seems to be doing all the running is actually a most wily
retriever, who ends up the winner by causing his hard-hitting adversary to make the errors. How? By using his head.

The 1963 U.S. Men's Singles Final was a perfect example of just
what I'm describing. Frank Froehling, from Miami, Florida, 6 feet 3,
was playing against Raphael Osuna, 5 feet 4, of Mexico. Froehling
has a big, powerful serve and a good follow-up volley. On paper, and
with his good summer record, it looked as though he had at least a
50-50 chance of winning. But little Osuna completely outwitted him.
Sometimes he stayed way back to receive serve, practically as far as
the stadium wall; sometimes he moved way up (much like the table-
tennis champions) . . . and he was quick enough to get away with

it. He would half-volley some returns with sharp angles or at Froehling's feet, and he'd lob others so deceptively that they were hard to anticipate. Poor Frank didn't know what to do and became so befuddled that he couldn't even get his big serve in—he had never run into anyone like this before. (The first time is always the toughest. I'll bet he would know how to handle the situation today.) The match went to Osuna in three straight sets. Cunning had won over brawn.

The conclusion I have drawn from watching and playing tournament tennis for over twenty-five years is that the ideal style is a combination of offense and defense. It's important to develop power and hard shots, if you have the physique to do it. So let's say you have the physique. Obviously power alone isn't enough, unless you can back it up with stroke-consistency and a good dash of brains. It's just as important to know when and how to defend; and, since there is a defense for almost every attack, you, with your physical assets, are in a capital position to acquire this elusive style, the style that balances offense and defense.

But will you? Your biggest problem in the beginning will probably be lack of patience. Since you're ambitious and competitive, you will try to make the winning shot too soon. You must learn to slow down, control your eagerness, and wait for an opening before shooting for the bull's-eye. Easier said than done, I know. Work hard on developing your ground strokes. (Use the same method of practicing as suggested for the noncompetitive players in the previous chapter—the cross-court shots, forehand and backhand, and the down-the-line shots.)

How do you think Don Budge became world's champion? Not only did he have the physique and the "big game," but he also had the sense to learn and develop wonderful ground strokes (the best backhand I ever saw). And he practiced and practiced endlessly, with patience. He also had a great coach, Tom Stow, from Berkeley, California, who recognized Don's potential and spent many, many hours working with him, believing in him, and helping to build his confidence in himself.

Many well-equipped players seem to have the potential of a Don Budge or a Jack Kramer but never get anywhere because they don't appreciate the value of sound ground strokes. They also don't realize the value of getting the first serve into play. I can't emphasize this

(Left) The great Don Budge could do practically anything with his backhand—hit it hard, soft, high or low. Here he is hitting a slightly undersliced volley, with both feet off the ground. *Eucom Special Services Photo.* (Right) Don Budge's coach, Tom Stow from Berkeley, California, helped me with my backhand. Here I am learning a new grip.

too much: in competitive play it makes the whole difference between being a mediocre or a good player. Getting your first serve in court not only gives you the opportunity to get up to the net quickly, but has a psychological effect on the receiver. It makes him think and act defensively; whereas, if you miss the first serve, he subconsciously gets the feeling of being the aggressor (even though your second serve is just as hard as your first), and the tide may turn to his advantage. *Don't give him this advantage: get your first serve in court.*

Any tournament player will tell you that this is true, and he will also tell you that the follow-up volley, as you run in after your serve, is one of the most difficult and important shots in winning a point. The better your serve, the easier the follow-up volley. In some instances, with a good first serve and a quick rush to the net, it can be a put-away volley. In others, you will have to settle for a well-placed first volley to force a weak return (or bad lob) for a put-away second volley. Never run in to the net after a feeble serve, unless you are a sensational volleyer or are playing against a dub.

You will learn best what you're capable of doing by using that old reliable formula, trial and error. And above all get as much tournament experience as possible, so that you find out what you can and can't do under pressure. So many players look superb in practice, and then they get in a match and seem to fall apart . . . their superb-looking shots manage to land anywhere but in court.

Now—how about you competitive ones who *don't* have the big physique? You will have to go about winning in quite a different way. Instead of *developing* the big game, you must learn how to *handle* the big game and the counterattack with even more guile than does your opponent. Your tactics will be more complicated, but all the more satisfactory when successful. One dampening thought—if your opponent can equal you in guile and has the big physique, too, I'm afraid you're licked. But don't let it stop you from trying, because you'll beat so many along the way. Remember, the chances are that most of them won't use their brains, because they aren't forced to. You, on the other hand, know that you have to.

Here are some of the things you can do: concentrate on improving your anticipation, speedy footwork, the art of placement and court position, the different spins, and how to break up your opponent's timing by using change of pace. For example, once you sense that he is having a good day, and his shots are consistently being hit hard (too hard for you), this is the time to break up his rhythm. Don't give him hard shots (on which he will thrive); instead, give him some "dinks," some drop shots, some wide angles, some soft poopy lobs deep to his backhand: anything to break up his good timing of the moment. Soon (you hope) he'll start worrying and pressing and making those welcome errors you've been waiting for.

The Successful Pattern

None of this, of course, entitles you to overlook the offense . . . not by a long shot. Your efforts will be wasted, if, when the opening comes, you're not ready to capitalize on it and force the issue—meaning that you should learn how to handle the short shots and have some put-away strokes of your own.

There are certain set tactics for all you competitors (large and small) that may be used to win points. Haven't you noticed how some

Peter Pan had nothing on Mrs. Billie Jean King, ranked number one in the United States jointly with Nancy Richey in 1966, stretching for a high forehand in Melbourne, Australia. *Australian News and Information Bureau Photograph by C. Bottomley.* Since then she has twice won the U.S. singles and three times Wimbledon and became the first lady athlete to earn over $100,000 prize money in a year.

players win by using what seem to be really simple tactics? I used to marvel at the ease with which Helen Wills won her matches. Even though I was only about thirteen years old at the time, I studied her strategy very carefully—I couldn't figure it out at first: she didn't seem to be doing anything so spectacular (although she had great power), yet somehow she made almost no errors, and her opponents did. Why? As I grew older, I began to understand and appreciate the reasons for her greatness—*she had a purpose in everything she did.* She had also a pattern, a fixed set of tactics, which she used against everyone—so well that she didn't need to resort to variety.

For instance her first serve was almost invariably in court, deep and well placed in one corner or the other. Her drives were likewise deep and well placed. She never started at too fast a pace; she worked up to it. The first few games were usually close and hard fought. Helen was apparently content to get her range and to tire her opponent by degrees, in a cat-and-mouse manner. At first she allowed herself plenty of margin but still managed to keep her opponent running from side to side—the rallies were long—and the pattern began to show itself. The pace of her shots gradually sped up; the rallies became shorter; the angles became more acute: one deep shot, one wide angle on the other side, then two vicious shots to the same side finally forced the opening for the winning placement. The poor "mouse" would begin to tire, and it was always just a question of time before the "cat" gobbled him up.

The reason this pattern worked so successfully was that Helen's shots carried such terrific pace and were so consistent and well aimed. Doubters of her greatness suggest that she could have been beaten by such volleyers and all-court players as Margaret Smith and Maria Bueno, and by those who might have run her up and back with drop shots and lobs. Well, I saw some girls, like Eleanor Goss and Marion Jessup, try to do just this in the 1920s (and don't think that some of

Arthur Ashe following through on a backhand drive. He must have been rushed, since he hasn't stepped forward on his right foot, but he kept his balance and his weight was going into the ball.

them weren't as good as the gals today), but it didn't work, at least not when Helen was at her peak. Naturally, when she slowed up and lost her great power, she began to suffer occasional losses.

Another great player who, in his amateur days, was able to use one pattern against almost all his opponents (or so it seemed on the surface) was Don Budge. His tactics looked fairly simple too. Like Helen, he started steadily, finding his range and running his opponent. But the minute he was able to force a weak or short return, he was on it in a flash, hitting the ball on the rise to one corner or the other and making such a good running-in shot that he usually had no more than an easy put-away volley or smash to make (not that he couldn't make a superb volley when he had to—especially on the backhand side). The closer the match, the more often he was in at the net, never relaxing that pressure.

Many of the champs of today, both pro and amateur, like Rod Laver, Roy Emerson and Arthur Ashe, have as good serves and volleys as Budge did, but their ground strokes are nowhere near so reliable. Little Ken Rosewall of Australia comes as near as any (or he did at his peak) to having the soundest ground strokes, and I have always felt that if he had been a few inches taller, so he would have had a more powerful serve, he could have been another Kramer or Gonzalez. I also feel that Arthur Ashe has the potential of developing into one of our all-time greats. He reminds me more of Pancho Gonzalez than of anyone else. Arthur also seems to have the heart and temperament to go along with his shots. In his extraordinary match against Roy Emerson, whom he upset in the quarterfinals of the 1965 Nationals, none of the ordinary annoyances (like bad line calls and bad bounces), bothered him. He showed himself to be a fine sport with lots of guts and good court manners.

Let's get back to you now, and how to help you have the most fun out of competitive tennis. The main thing for you to decide is the kind of player you want to be; also the kind you are best suited for, temperamentally and physically. Once you get a clear picture in your mind, then you are in a position to decide the kind of strategy you plan to use: you are ready to explore the ways and means, or tactics, by which you will carry out your campaign.

8 · TACTICS: SINGLES AND DOUBLES

Here are some hints, actually fundamentals, that should help you win matches, whether in a family match, a tournament, or just against that boastful rival.

SINGLES TACTICS

We'll begin with singles. You find yourself on the court facing one opponent. If you have ever played against him before, or have watched him play, you will at least know what to expect from him. If not, you must try to find out as much about him as you can during the rallying or warming-up period before the match begins. Find out for instance which is his stronger and which his weaker side, the forehand or the backhand (he'll usually let you know this by standing over to favor his good side). Find out whether his strokes are offensive or defensive. And, if one side does seem to be more offensive, perhaps it's also more erratic. If so, don't forget it. Notice his footwork—is he fast or slow, alert or lazy? Has he a big roundhouse swing that demands plenty of room and time, or does he rush his shots and get impatient with a soft floater? Naturally you can't find out all these things in your warm-up period, but do try to observe as much as you can. The rest will show itself soon enough as the match progresses.

While observing your opponent, try to get your own strokes going smoothly. If you didn't get a chance to hit some balls before the match (most tournament players rally on another court for ten or fifteen minutes before a big match), now is the time to loosen the muscles and swing with a rhythmical, relaxed feeling. This will help any nervous tension you may have, as well as get the strokes going. Once the match starts, you'll be much too busy thinking of *where* to hit the ball to worry about *how* to hit it (or should be anyway).

As you get under way, spend the first few games finding your range (like Helen Wills and Don Budge—remember?) In other words, allow plenty of margin: don't aim as close to the net or to the lines as you usually do in practice. And forget once and for all any idea that you are out there to blast your opponent off the court. Many players have fallen prey to this tantalizing thought, but it very seldom works and can lead to a downfall. Get your range first and make sure of your consistency . . . then you can pour it on at will when you're ready.

If you win the toss it is usual to choose to serve first, and your opponent gets to choose the side of the court. Since you change courts on the odd game, that is, after the first, third, fifth, etc., you should select the worst side first, with the sun facing you smack in the face, or with a strong wind blowing hard against you. In this way you'll get one more game on the good side. That one game may win you a set. There are times when you may choose to receive instead of serve, especially if you don't have a particularly formidable serve and your opponent does. I sometimes did this if I was playing someone like Louise Brough or Doris Hart, who had big serves—the reason being that you can often break through their serve on the very first game, before they are quite confident or sufficiently warmed up. Then if you can hold your own, it too may mean the set.

All right—you have won the toss and have elected to serve. You should concentrate all your energies on getting the first serve in court, and on keeping the first and second serves as nearly alike as possible. Anything to avoid a poopy little second serve which your opponent, if he's any good at all, can deal with as he likes. He'll have such a beautiful array of choices that you'll find it tough to anticipate which one he has chosen and, consequently, will find yourself helpless. Concentrate also on serving to your opponent's weakness, if he has one. If he starts running around the ball in order to hit it on his strong side, serve to him on his strong side—very wide. This should keep him over where he belongs—for a while at least.

When you receive, watch the ball carefully, not merely when your opponent hits it, but actually while he is tossing it in the air: you can tell a great deal from the toss as to what kind of a serve is coming, whether a slice, a flat serve or an American twist. Every second of warning is precious time saved. The first essential in returning serve is to keep the ball in play—don't try to do more than you think you can; the second is to return it as far from your opponent as possible. I can still hear Mrs. Wightman's familiar words to us youngsters, "Put the ball where the other fellow *isn't*." Easier said than done, as you'll soon find out. Sometimes it's all you can do just to get the ball back. Try at least to return it deep, so that your opponent can't start forcing right away. A deep return, either hard or soft (preferably to the backhand, unless you're playing a Don Budge or a Pauline Betz), is a good reliable shot except against a player who runs in to the net behind his serve. If he's a net rusher, give him low short returns, which will catch him at his feet or a wide angle. A good lob is often effective, too . . . high to the backhand.

After making your return of serve, get back into position quickly. Above all, don't stand entranced, as do most beginners, waiting to see where your shot goes. If it's really so fine that you can't help admiring it, at least learn to admire and move at the same time.

Your best position in singles is in the middle of the court, a foot or so behind the base line, depending on your size, reach, and fleetness of foot. You should establish yourself here or up at the net. Try not to get caught in between, in no-man's-land, the territory between the service line and the base line. Getting caught here means that you will have to be an expert at the low volley or the half volley (hitting the ball on the rise just after it bounces). Not many players can afford to spend much time in this region. A few have been able to get away with it . . . Henri Cochet, Dick Williams, Raphael Osuna, Maria Bueno, to name some . . . but not really by choice. Since they weren't tall, they couldn't get too close to the net on account of lobs; therefore they were forced to develop that halfway-up shot—not to be recommended for the average player.

Mrs. Pauline Betz Addie, former Wimbledon Champion and four-time winner of the United States National Singles, had one of the great backhands in women's tennis. Here she is seen following through after a low backhand drive.

The Running-In Shot

The moment to launch a net attack of your own is when your obliging opponent inadvertently hits you a short shot, one which lands near the service line. The higher the bounce, the easier your approach shot will be, because you'll be hitting down on it and will be able to choose whether to hit a deep shot or an angle. A low bounce, below the level of the net, gives you less of an option, since it is almost impossible to hit it deep and keep it in court. Wiser methods are to cut it back low, angle it to one side, or even try for a drop shot. But remember: when the ball lands short, either waist high or over, don't hesitate to hit it on the rise, or as near the top of the bounce as possible, thus giving your opponent less time to recover his position. You needn't hit this running-in shot very hard either. If you meet the ball squarely, with your body weight coming into the ball (without beveling the face of your racket at the moment of impact), you will hardly ever miss. Surprised? Try it and see.

A straight down-the-line running-in shot is almost always more successful than a cross-court one. The distance up to the net is shorter for you, and, once there, you will be in a better position to handle your opponent's attempted passing shot. If he tries the straight-line passing shot, you'll be right there waiting for it. If he tries the cross-court one, he'll have to try for a risky wide angle and won't be giving himself much margin of safety.

There are times when other running-in shots are wiser: if you have forced your opponent way out of position on one side of the court, you should obviously hit your running-in shot to the other; if your opponent has a glaring weakness, you should obviously shoot for that; and you ought to experiment with the "center-court theory." Some players have trouble, when a ball comes directly at them, making up their minds quickly on which side to pass you. The strategy of hitting the ball straight down the middle works well against those with an exceptionally good cross-court shot, which you're not giving them a chance to use. On the other hand it leaves you with a large expanse of court to cover on both sides—as well as a lob to watch out for, so I shouldn't advise this as a regular practice. Do give it a try when and if the occasion seems right.

Another useful running-in shot is a deep chop. Since it travels more slowly than a drive, a chop will give you more time to get to a good position at the net. However it will also give your opponent more time to pass you, if he is capable of handling chops. Many players aren't. Find out whether he is or isn't . . . then decide accordingly.

Still another kind of running-in shot, which may work well under certain circumstances, is the short shot. I know this may sound contrary to your instincts, but let's say that you're playing against a boringly steady player (rather slow footed), who stands well behind the base line. You can catch him when he's way back on one side with a short running-in shot on the other side. He'll have to hit up, if he gets there at all, and all you will have to do is put the ball away.

Are there any other occasions when it's wise to run in? Yes: when you can frighten a nervous opponent by the sheer audacity of any kind of a net attack, whether it's judicious or not. You'd be surprised how often you can force an error just by tearing up to the net as though you knew what you were doing (your opponent doesn't know that you don't). One other equally daring assault may work when your opponent himself is a net rusher: you can steal his thunder by getting there first and hogging the net yourself. You'll only be able to do this safely if, like some net rushers, he's weak on ground strokes; you, obviously, must also be a good volleyer.

To summarize: Run in when your opponent hits a weak or short return, remembering that the success of your net attack is bound to depend tremendously on your actual running-in shot. Take no unnecessary chances with it. Above all don't aim too close to the lines: leave some margin—at least a yard. Follow your shot in as close to the net as you can safely go and still be able to cover a lob.

Volleying at Net

Once you're up at the net and ready to volley, where should you aim the ball? It goes without saying that you should hit the volley as far away from your opponent as possible. If he's on one side, aim for the other. If he's way back, volley short. If he's in the middle, you can angle your volley wide to either side. A drop volley is a delicate but effective shot. The most difficult volley to make is an extremely low one, when your opponent has caught you at your feet. In this unfortunate situation you must aim low over the net (more on just how to do this in the chapter on strokes). If you make the mistake of volleying up, you'll be entirely at his mercy.

The Passing Shot

Now let's consider the net attack from the opposite point of view. What do you do when your opponent runs in against you? For example: What should you do when you are the one who has made the weak return? You have three possibilities (depending of course on the kind of running-in shot he makes): you can try to pass him outright, you can lob over his head, or you can hit a short low ball to his feet. If he has made a forceful running-in shot and is securely established at the net, it would be difficult, but not impossible, for you to pass him. The best time to try passing is when the running-in shot has not been especially strong and you see an opening to aim for. Do so. Your passing shot, once you decide to use it, should be hit as low as possible, and (if you know how) with a bit of top spin or dip, which will make it more difficult for your opponent to handle, even if he reaches it.

A straight-line passing shot is usually easiest for you to make with accuracy and severity, although a sharp angle can be equally successful if more difficult to execute (you have less space to aim for).

There are alternatives to the passing shots. Try a good lob (if you make a bad one, you might as well kiss the point good-by), preferably over his head, when your opponent is crowding the net; but hit your lob with real firmness and authority—don't baby it. If your opponent hangs back, perhaps anticipating a lob, hit a low one towards his ankles in hopes that he'll be forced to volley up and allow you to pass him on the next shot.

When should you run in on your serve? Probably only when you get a good first serve in deep to your opponent's backhand, or wide to his forehand. Not many players have a good enough second serve to follow it in. If you do, go ahead. As I mentioned before, the element of surprise is the main objective for you when running in on the serve. Therefore vary your pattern so that your opponent doesn't have a chance to get set. Also vary the pace—don't always hit your cannonball (if you're lucky enough to have one). Bill Tilden and Alice

(Above) Santana's opponent, with back to the camera, has very little choice if he reaches this low forehand volley: he must either aim the ball just over the net for a drop volley, or chop a low deep volley to Santana's backhand, a difficult shot to make.

(Left) Mrs. Billie Jean King making a straight line passing shot. Obviously she is shooting for a winner, since she is being forced so far out of court she won't have time to get back. *World Tennis Magazine.*

Marble used to save theirs for the important times when they *had* to win the point.

What should you do when your opponent runs in on his serve? Your choices are much the same as they were against his good running-in ground stroke, or approach shot. Either try to pass him (down the line or cross court); lob over his head (preferably on the backhand side); or hit the ball at his shoelaces as he runs in. One other possible winner, if you possess a forceful drive and if you're the daring type, is to hit your return smack at him—in the area of his midsection. Some people have trouble getting out of their own way.

Managing the Back-Court Player

So far I've been emphasizing the winning of points through volleying. Not all opponents are volleyers of course. You may find that you are up against a back-court player who shows clearly that he can (and plans to) outsteady you from the base line. This is often the case in junior public parks and club tournaments, where feverishly competitive players will do anything to win a match. These pesky pluggers seem to be able to keep the ball in play all day long, running tirelessly, looping, chopping, lunging, digging. Instead of letting your opponent's steadiness irk or discourage you, ask yourself why he plays this kind of game. Could he be doing it by choice? Most likely not. He probably doesn't have the approach shots to get him to the net; and, once there, he probably isn't much of a volleyer. Your strategy, therefore, should be to lure him up to the net, whether he likes it or not. To accomplish this foxy maneuver, vary your deep shots with deliberately short returns and with occasional drop shots. This scheme will work of course only if your short shot is really short and low. Otherwise you will simply have handed your opponent an easy setup to put away.

Change of Length and Other Defenses

Change of length bothers many people, especially girls. What also tires an opponent is a wide angle. This was one of Suzanne Lenglen's specialties. (She was the great French champion of the early 1920's and, in some people's opinion, the greatest woman tennis player of all time.) Her angle shot was tantalizingly soft and wide, followed by a hard, deep shot to the other side. I was very young when I saw her play on her professional tour and don't remember her very well; but I can easily believe the accounts of her remarkable accuracy. Apparently she could aim at a very small square on the court and hit it. When she was a girl, her father trained her to do this by dropping handkerchiefs in different locations and paying her the equivalent of a quarter whenever she hit one of the linen squares.

I have already mentioned change of pace and variety as helpful ways of winning points. There's another situation you should know about and be able to handle. That's when you find yourself opposite a player who has one outstanding, forceful shot. Your instinct will tell you to keep away from that shot at all costs and concentrate on his other, more defensive side. This is not always the right thing to do. It's wise to experiment a little, because sometimes a player's defense may be steadier than his offense, and he'll actually make more errors on his strong side. By giving his weak side too much practice during the match, you may even end by improving it. Your smarter course may be to play right to his strength, waiting for the strategic moment to hit one to his weakness when he's not prepared for it. These same tactics can be applied to an opponent who starts running around his weakness in order to hit the ball on his good side. Hit wide to his strength—the wider the better—leaving more space for your next shot to his vulnerable weak side.

The only time this doesn't work is in a strong wind. What troubles I had at the Maidstone Club in Easthampton, Long Island, playing a match against Dorothy (Dodo) Bundy of the famous Sutton family from California, with her strong Western forehand and a crosswind behind her! Try as I could, it was almost impossible to put any shot wide to her backhand, because the wind would blow it near enough the middle that she could run around it and whack her forehand to my defenseless backhand. It was all right when we changed courts and I had the wind behind me; but it wasn't fun, and I always prayed for a windless day when I met Dodo in a tournament thereafter.

When you find yourself outmaneuvered and on the run (your opponent having forced you way out of court), there are two possibilities open to you. One is to lob a great high ball, which will give you time to recover your position while you hope that your opponent doesn't have a good overhead. The other is to shoot for an outright winner, with no thought of getting back into position. Since you're in trouble anyway, you may as well shoot the works and aim for the most available opening. In other words, any shot that can be returned won't help you: you need an ace.

I have a suggestion if you're aiming for a down-the-line shot. If your opponent has pulled you way out to one side, you must allow quite a bit more margin on your straight shot than you ordinarily would, because the weight of your moving body plus the angle of the ball will draw a shot aimed anywhere near the line out of court. (This applies to your running-in and passing shots also.)

Ordinarily you shouldn't try for a winner from the back court unless you have forced your opponent out of position. You must be content to wait for an opening.

DOUBLES TACTICS

What I have said so far about tactics applies specifically to singles. Let's turn our attention now to the game of doubles, which involves a whole new set of principles. You may have supposed that doubles was approximately the same game as singles—except that there were two players on each side, and a wider court with doubles alleys added. Right . . . up to a point. But the strategy is completely different. The game becomes faster; the volleying is more important; anticipation and quick reflexes are paramount; the angles and placements of the shots are different. To be more specific, the physical aspect of the court changes considerably when it's occupied by two players instead of one. The openings, so large and inviting in singles, are no longer there. It takes cleverness, finesse and, above all, teamwork to find, or make, the new and smaller openings.

The Team and How It Works

The two players should work as a coordinated unit, each aware of what his partner is going to do and which balls his partner is going to hit, and where. This is far from easy: it requires quick thinking. You may reason that each player should just cover his own side of the court, but it doesn't always work that way. There are times when there are doubtful shots: the ones down the middle (when one player

"Occasionally both players say 'mine' at the same moment . . ." This was the finals of Wimbledon in 1939, which Alice Marble and I won for the second time. I don't remember which one of us actually hit the ball—but we were both going for it. *Copyright British Press Combine.*

has to cover his alley) or up in the air (when one player is in a better position to put the ball away even though it's on the other player's side)—difficult decisions to be made fast. The calling of "yours" and "mine" is a good habit for one to acquire. Mrs. Wightman taught me this when I was ten. The player who decides first, because he is in a better position to decide, becomes master of the situation and gives his partner the necessary information.

Let's say for instance that you're standing close to the net (expecting a shot down the middle), and your opponent surprises you with a sudden lob which you realize immediately you won't be able to reach. If you yell, "Yours," to your partner right away and cross over to the other side, you'll at least give him a chance to get to the lob. Maybe he will, maybe he won't, but you will have given him a few precious seconds of warning.

Usually the player on the left side takes the doubtful middle shots, whether low ones or lobs, because they are on his forehand. It still prevents confusion if he says, "Mine," before reaching for the doubt-

ful ones. Occasionally both players say, "Mine," at the same moment
and then collide. But this doesn't happen often. It's better for this
to happen occasionally than to have both players cry, "Yours," at
the same time, and let the ball sail serenely through.

There are times when the player on the left side is in a poor position to take a middle shot. If, for instance, his partner serves or hits
a wide cross-court shot to his opponent's forehand, the man on the
left must step over toward his alley to cover a straight-line passing
shot. He leaves the center for his partner to cover. There are also
times when the man who has hit the last shot should take the next
middle one because, pursuing the direction of his own shot, he is
better able to anticipate where the return will come.

Obviously you can't play first-class doubles, either in social tennis
or tournament competition, unless you can volley. As strong ground
strokes are a necessity in singles, so volleys are in doubles. Once the
ball is put in play, most of the hitting is done up at the net. The two
members of a top-notch team, when they take the net, form an almost
impregnable battle line. So the sooner you and your partner together
can reach the net, the better. If one of you is up and one back, against
a pair already at the net, your opponents will be able to shoot fast
into the gaps between you. Run in, therefore, whenever you can.
Run in on your serve (if it's any good); run in on your return of serve
(unless the return is lousy), or on the first shot afterward that seems
good enough.

There are bound to be times when all four players are at the net
together in a cozy little foursome. It's in these situations that you need
a steady head, quick reflexes and a stout heart. Remember the basic

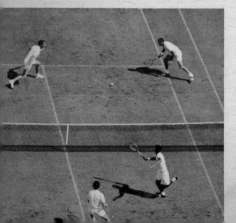

This match was one of tennis-
dom's big upsets. Alex Olmedo
(near side of net) puts a backhand volley through a small gap,
as he and his partner, Ham
Richardson, defeated Neale
Fraser (left far court) and Mal
Anderson of Australia in 1958 in
one of the longest Davis Cup
matches in history. *Australian
News and Information Bureau
Photograph by J. Tanner.*

principles: keep cool and alert; expect every ball to come to you; raise your racket and block the ball in front of you; aim it as low over the net as possible. Nothing is more exciting to both players and spectators, nothing is more fun to watch, than a fast exchange of this kind between four first-class volleyers. It's great!

The Serve and Return of Serve

Once again we must emphasize the importance of the first serve: If you plan to reach the net successfully in doubles, your *two most vital shots* are the first serve and the return of serve. You must learn to control them. A well-placed, medium-hard serve in doubles, even the first one, is more effective than a fast one (unless it's an ace or so good it forces a weak return), because it gives you more time to get to the net. If you miss your first serve, your problems increase. Unless your second serve is reliably deep or high kicking, one which really forces an opponent back, you must expect to be punished for missing the first one. You'll find yourself in the uncomfortable position of having to choose between running in on the weak serve, and probably getting caught with a ball at your feet or with one too hard to handle. The alternative is to stay back, which will force you into the one-up-one-back arrangement that will allow your opponents to take the offensive. My advice is to run in anyway. It's the lesser of two evils—and perhaps your opponent won't make as good a return as you fear.

Another drawback to missing the first serve is the wasted effort. The strength it takes to run halfway in, put on the brakes, walk back, serve, and run in again tires you unnecessarily. How much more tiring it seems to serve a fault than an ace! The former fatigues you while the latter exhilarates, even though you use the same body motion. And a double fault can be positively exhausting.

The court position of the server in doubles differs slightly from his position in singles. In the right court it's about the same—he should stand near the middle and aim to his opponent's backhand. This will always hold true unless the opponent has an unusually good backhand or weak forehand, because the backhand return of the receiver in the right court is one of the most difficult shots in tennis doubles. It either has to be an aggressive down-the-middle shot; a right-to-left angle to the server's forehand; or a lob over the net man's head—all three very tough to make.

But, and here's a big difference from singles, when serving to the opponent on the left side, you (the server) may stand way over to the left of center—in fact, close to the alley lines. In this way you can serve to your opponent's backhand since your partner is up at the net and can (you hope) handle the middle returns, while you cover the cross-court angle. I don't mean to imply that the server must aim to the opponent's backhand on every serve. Naturally he must vary his direction from time to time with, perhaps, a wide forehand in the first court and a down-the-center forehand in the second. But the percentage of winning points is higher on the backhand side.

The best position for the server's partner, obviously, is up at the net. From there he can cut off all weak returns with sharp volleys, and by his very presence at the net he can sometimes force an opponent, fearful of the net man's poaching, to try for a wider return than he ought. (More on this subject in the "Gamesmanship" chapter.) "Poaching" is what it sounds like: jumping across into your partner's territory, volleying the shot intended for him, and putting the ball away. If you make it, you'll win kudos; if you muff it, you're a bum. It must be done quickly and expertly or not at all, so, unless you're pretty sure that you can complete your mission and actually put the ball away, you had better be satisfied to guard your own side capably.

Dennis Ralston, number one United States player in 1964 and 1965, up at the net guarding his side, while his partner, Chuck McKinley, 1963 Wimbledon Singles Champion, and three-time winner of the United States National Men's Doubles with Ralston, gets ready to receive serve.

By crossing over, you may bother your partner, unless you both have a working formula, because it disrupts the formation of the team. It may even start a civil war.

To guard your side capably, when your partner is serving, you should stand just to the left of the middle of your half of the court. With one quick step and a jump, starting with the left foot and landing on the right, you ought to be able to reach your alley shots with a backhand volley—a shot for which you should always be on the alert. And with a quick step and leap the other way (starting with the right foot and landing on the left) you can cover your shots down the middle with a forehand volley. The distance you stand back from the net depends on your height and your ability to handle the lobs which are your responsibility.

To guard your side when your partner is receiving and you are up at the net, stand a little farther back and nearer the middle. This way you can protect that vulnerable middle hole if your partner's return of serve is poor. Your opponent, your vis-à-vis up at the net, with his partner serving, will be ready to shoot diagonally through this hole if he can get his racket on the ball. You can help thwart this plan if you expect it.

Because of this possibility, some players prefer not to stand at the net when their partner receives, especially if he doesn't have a good return of serve or is having a bad day. The alternative is to stay back with your partner, on the base line or just inside, ready to run in with him if his return is good enough. (Caution—be ready for short or drop volleys.) If your opponent's serve is so good that your partner is forced to make a defensive return, you will both stay back and play the point with "offensive" defense, by alternating low dipping shots at your opponents' feet with good lobs over their heads, hoping to make them miss their volleys or smashes.

The importance of the return of serve in doubles cannot be over-emphasized. It has turned the tide in many a match. In top-flight tennis it's taken for granted that the server ought to win his serve, because then his team can get to the net first and take the offensive. (I am well aware that you won't be able to accomplish this every time.) The team that can hold its own service need break through the op-

posing team's service *just once* per set to win that set. The return of
serve is the shot that paves the way for this one breakthrough. If
the return is good enough it can wrest the offensive away from the
server and force him to volley up.

There are several choices for good return of service, and they depend considerably on your ability to handle the serve. The best position for the receiver is near the base line, perhaps even inside it, because, the sooner he is able to hit the ball, the greater his chance of
hitting it low at his opponent, who is on his way to the net. This position also decreases his distance to the net, if he decides his return is
good enough to follow to the net, and allows the server less time to
get to the net. However, standing inside the base line is not easy for
the average player since it means hitting the ball on the rise (before
it reaches the top of the bounce), and this takes good timing and experience. So until you find out what your capabilities are, it will be
more sensible for you to stand farther back to start with and gradually work your way up as you improve. It's really a question of being
more alert, anticipating faster, and taking a shorter back swing.

Ordinarily your return should be aimed at the server, because he is
in a poorer position to volley and less well balanced (after serving
and running in) than his partner, who is comfortably ensconced at the
net and, supposedly, alert. Keep your return as low as possible and
aim at the server's ankles as he comes in; or make a dipping shot
down the center of the court that his partner can't intercept; or hit a
wide cross-court angle. Sometimes when a serve is very good you
haven't time to aim so accurately. Try then to surprise the server with
a fast ball right at him or with an unexpected lob. And if the server's
partner seems to be edging his way too far towards the center, don't
neglect an occasional shot down his alley or a lob over his head. You
really have lots of choices of returns of serve, and it's up to you to
decide which is the right one for the occasion.

I've been describing the game of doubles as it should be played by
top-notch teams. But you may very possibly feel that you're not
capable of running in to the net as often as I've suggested. This
doesn't mean you can't have fun out of the game of doubles. If you
get the "timing jitters" up at the net, stay in the back court and de-

velop the defensive tactics with pleasure and profit, upsetting your opponent's wits by alternating drives, low dipping shots and lobs.

Anticipation and Concentration

As time goes on you will gradually become familiar with these tactics. The strategy of both singles and doubles will become second nature to you. Best of all you will find yourself having more time because you will be developing anticipation—the magic word in tennis. A great champion, through constant practice and experience, knows where your shots are going almost before you make them. The techniques of court mastery become instinctive and guesswork is reduced to a minimum. What may look to you like a player's inspired guess is really trained memory and developed anticipation. But anticipation is fickle—it ebbs and flows. Just lay off tennis for a while and you will find it has temporarily deserted you. It can be recaptured only by renewed effort. Some people are born with more anticipation than others; nevertheless, it can be cultivated to a large extent, and this is well worthwhile, as it will provide one of the great satisfactions in tennis.

One last bit of advice is to concentrate on "concentration." I know that sounds funny, but it's exactly what I mean. By putting your mind on concentration, you'll be making great strides towards winning at tennis. It is a most vital quality that is often not properly evaluated. Good tennis demands it constantly, not just at critical moments but throughout the match. It's extraordinary how many matches are lost through lack of concentration. You will notice with the best players that concentration is a good deal more than the negative refusal to be bothered by obvious distractions: it's a positive process of shutting out everything extraneous. Through conscious effort, you can actually train your eyes and mind not to wander off the tennis court during a point. Pretty soon it will become a habit which you can accomplish without strain. This doesn't mean that you have to behave like a mechanical robot once the point or game is over—but when the ball is in play, you will "unplug the world" outside those white lines. There's more on this subject in the "Gamesmanship" chapter.

Now you are all set to compete at tennis and beat your opponent (or opponents) unmercifully.

9 · FITNESS AND CARE OF THE BODY

No matter what kind of tennis you have selected to play, whether it's to be aggressive, conservative, competitive or social, your body must be fit in order to do justice to it. For your own well-being and enjoyment, as well as for your game, learn *now* how to use and attend to your body. It will stand you in good stead the rest of your life. Not only will staying in condition help your tennis game, but it will enliven your everyday existence as well.

I was delighted to read the other day about an old lady in Texas who can still touch the floor with her fingers without bending her knees, as she demonstrated at her one-hundred-and-fifth birthday celebration.

You may be sure that this lady must have given thought to the care of her body during all those years. You must also agree that in the successful space flights, despite the utmost bravery and skill of the pilots, the real unheralded hero was the human body.

I'm not intimating that you necessarily want to live to be one hundred and five years old, or be a space pilot—but it's reassuring to know that, if you train and understand the body, you might be able to.

Exercises

I have been told by experts that tennis exercises more different parts of the body than any other sport (except wrestling and swimming—and who wants to be a wrestler?). Since exercise strongly affects muscles, it goes without saying that tennis exercise helps tremendously in the control and development of the various muscles.

No doubt you have read articles on physical fitness and have had the subject drummed into your head at school and by your parents. We read about how unfit the average youth of America really is today, compared to that of other nations. Statistics seem to bear this out, so we may as well accept the fact and decide to do something about it, rather than bury our heads in the sand. Being an enthusiastic believer in fitness myself, and having observed and experimented first hand for years, I am strongly of the opinion that fitness is attainable

106

to all (health permitting of course). And the way to fitness is nowhere near as complicated as most articles would lead you to believe. In other words, the correct simple exercises done *regularly,* as automatically as brushing your teeth morning and night, are much more beneficial than a complex series of exercises for each part of the body. So few people have the time or patience to follow the latter.

The ones I suggest are extremely easy; they don't take more than fifteen minutes in the morning and another fifteen in the evening— and they will help both your tennis and your physique. What more can you ask for? I've been doing them for twenty years and haven't changed more than two inches or two pounds in any direction (except when I was having my two children).

The first exercise begins immediately on waking in the morning. It's one you can do lying on your back. After I'm semiconscious and have stretched and yawned like a cat, I do five or six deep-breathings. (More details on breathing later.) By then I'm almost conscious, and ready for the first exercise. Slowly I raise my right leg and pedal an imaginary bicycle; then slowly do the same with the left leg. As I begin to feel a little action I speed up a bit; then it's time to rotate the two legs in synchronization. I complete twenty pedals with both legs, as rhythmically as possible. By this time (four minutes) I'm fully conscious.

After the face-wash, the teeth-brush, and the hair-comb, it's time for the second exercise, the one where you reach down with your fingers to touch your toes without bending your knees (which you should be able to do at age one hundred and five). I start this one slowly and loosely, letting my arms flop down like a gorilla's as I bend forward, but then stretching them high over my head on the upswing, as though trying to grow another half inch. Gradually I increase the tempo and discover that it gets easier each time, and I can reach lower. Twenty times in all—and rhythmically again. (Four minutes.)

The next exercise can be done either now or after breakfast (not directly after, however), depending on how energetic you feel. It's the leg-raising one, when you lie prone on a carpet (or mat) with your arms out at your sides, and your spine as flat to the ground as possible. Raise your legs straight up, with feet together, and lower them slowly to the floor. This is tough at first, and you'll find that you can do only three or four in the beginning. You can really feel the pull in the stomach muscles. The slower you do it, the better, the last few inches off the ground being the hardest. I do ten of these each session. (Three minutes.) You may prefer to start with one leg at a time, and build up to two.

My last daily exercise may make you smile: it's merely picking up my tennis racket in my right hand and swinging it twenty times each for the serve, the forehand, and the backhand—as though I were hitting an imaginary ball—then the same thing with my *left* arm, so that I don't get lopsided and overly developed on the right. (Four minutes.)

And that's all. A total of fifteen minutes.

Of course you may add as many other exercises as you wish—the more the merrier—and move to music, which will relieve boredom and help rhythm. What I have given you is a good basic start to which you should have no trouble sticking, day after day, and year after year.

Many players find that jumping rope improves footwork. Alice Marble was a dedicated skip-rope jumper. Walking on your hands is great if you can do it. My sister Mianne and I used to spend many happy hours upside down, walking around the school gym on our hands, much to the amusement of our classmates. Standing on the head is good, too—and less taxing.

Try chin-ups on a bar—they're excellent for your wrist and arm muscles. But get a bar that is high enough so that your toes don't touch the ground. Otherwise you'd be tempted to give yourself a little extra push to get started, which would destroy the whole purpose. Start with four or five chin-ups, placing the palms of your hands towards you, and ending with your chin over the bar. Increase the number of chin-ups by degrees.

Running, of course, is one of the best body trainers there is. The Australian players are active believers in the important advantages of running as an aid in strengthening the leg muscles, as well as the lungs. Guided by their captain, Harry Hopman, the Australian Davis

The Australian men players are not the only ones who take their training seriously. Here is Champion Margaret Smith Court doing some pretty fine double-knee jumps.

Cup Team undergoes a more rigorous training program than that of any other country's team. Besides playing tennis three or four hours a day the boys run at least three miles, lift fifty-pound weights, then do over two hundred and fifty successive double knee jumps. This strenuous routine doesn't take place just before Wimbledon, or the important national championships, or the Davis Cup matches. They're at it for at least nine months out of the year. No wonder they're so great. Billie Jean Moffitt King once said they eat overheads for breakfast and half volleys for lunch.

I don't recommend all this exercise for you just now, but if you do make the Junior Davis Cup or Wightman Cup squad, you'll find you not only need it but will enjoy it. One very important thing to remember about exercise is *always start slowly*. Active exercise should be preceded by warming-up exercises, which should be rhythmical and gentle in order to avoid undue strain and to ease any muscle tension. The tenser you are (especially before competing in a match), the more warm-ups you need. Turn on a popular-music record to make your warm-ups more relaxing and to help you exercise your muscles in *rhythm*. Warm muscles are less prone to injury and charley horses.

Breathing

To get the most out of these multiple exercises, you should know about breathing, which is more crucial than eating. Your body can survive for almost a month without food, but not more than four minutes without oxygen. You probably know that it's better to breathe in through the nose, which filters some of the impurities, and expel the air from the nose (the mouth may be used at certain times). I don't want to sound too clinical, but there is a right way of breathing that will help you in all your forms of exercise, especially tennis. You can improve your lung capacity by practicing correct breathing, the way opera singers do. Inhale deeply, way down to the diaphragm (pushing out the stomach as you do so) with shoulders back; hold your breath for a few seconds; then exhale gradually but thoroughly. Do this a few times every morning and at other times during the day, and try to do it rhythmically. You will be surprised how much less winded you'll feel during any type of physical exertion as time goes on.

The correct breathing procedure is not difficult to learn, once you understand it. You may miss many shots and wonder why, thinking you didn't watch the ball properly. This may have been true, but watching the ball and breathing are closely associated, since both are dependent on oxygen. Have you noticed that players often miss easy setups after long rallies? Or that a player frequently misses a soft shot after a series of fast exchanges? In each case the breathing rhythm ran counter to the stroking rhythm. You may have breathed in when you should have breathed out, or vice versa. This would account for your being bothered by the change of pace, which you didn't know how to counteract.

For all shots you should breathe in before you make the stroke, hold your breath during the back swing, and exhale slowly during the actual hitting of the ball and the follow-through. Don't breathe in through the mouth unless you have to. You will learn to time your breathing to the speed of the shot you're making. The slower the stroke, the deeper you inhale. With a volley, for instance, you should take only a short breath, hold it an instant, and expel it quickly. But be sure to expel the breath after you hit the ball—don't hoard the air.

Training

There are other aspects of physical fitness that are essential to match play. (Naturally these don't apply as much to the noncompetitor, but they will be beneficial in any case.) The laws of training are no more than plain common sense. To keep the body at its approximate best, regular hours of sleep are necessary. Otherwise the following day the body will be sluggish, and the mind as well. I'm not saying that you should get to bed by eleven o'clock every night, but I am saying that, if you are playing a match the next day and are serious about playing well, you should try to get eight hours of sleep the night before, or at least the amount that you need to feel rested. Some require more sleep than others (I used to need nine hours).

Whatever they are, your sleeping habits shouldn't be spasmodic, to be applied only when you have an important game coming up. They should become customary. You alone must be the one to figure out what's best for you and act accordingly. As in all fields of endeavor, some pleasures have to be sacrificed for the sake of success. It's up to you to weigh the values and try to achieve a nice balance. So, if you're taking your date to the school dance on Friday night and have the finals of a club tournament to play the next morning—that's your problem.

A certain amount of mental relaxation is absolutely necessary for a competitive player. Budge and Mako used to play records of swing music—oh, how they played swing records. You may prefer bridge, poker, concerts, museums, reading, dancing, or just plain conversation. Whatever it is, it's good to have a diversion from tennis. Too much tennis without relaxation can cause staleness, or mental fatigue.

The three things to avoid just before playing a match are swimming (it relaxes the limbs too much), watching movies (possible eyestrain), and eating a heavy meal (it can make you feel miserable).

Obviously, excesses of any kind do you no good. You've got to use some willpower even to come close to reaching your potential. Don't let yourself down.

Diet

Speaking of excesses, food can be the number-one contender for top honors. It's so easy to fall into bad eating habits. I have always resented the fact that habits are so easy to form and so hard to break, a most unfair state of affairs. Eating habits seem to be the worst. Maybe that's because we start them so young. As I think back on my days as a teenager, I regret that I didn't know then what I know now. Those many afternoons when those of us with any spare cash in our pockets would stop at the drugstore on our way home from school and gorge ourselves with the most outlandish banana splits, double chocolate sodas, gooey candy bars—how could we! Needless to say these self-indulgent habits played havoc with our figures, our teeth and our complexions. Once we started dating and caring about our appearance, the habit subsided. Of course it should never have started —but we were too dumb (or deaf, I should say) and shortsighted to listen to anyone who gave us sensible advice.

Good diet habits and tastes are as easy to form as bad ones, and you won't have to break them later. Once you develop a craving for something, and have once given into it, it can be sheer agony to cut it out. As with exercise, there's no substitute for common sense. No one is going to give you his: you've got to use your own.

Common sense will tell you to eat well but in moderation; it will tell you to eat well-balanced meals that supply the necessary body-building nutrients and vitamins, and to go very easy on fats, fried foods, carbohydrates and sweets. This doesn't mean giving them up entirely (I know you won't anyway), and a certain amount of sugar is needed for energy—but you must learn to control the amount and want less. And, to quote a phrase, "Calories do count." It's worth your while to study a calorie chart and memorize the somewhat-surprising results. I almost never have to refer to mine now, since I know by heart how many calories are in a slice of bread, an apple, a frankfurter, a piece of pumpkin pie, a glass of milk. Consequently I have no problem making my decisions promptly.

Tennis players, like all athletes, need plenty of hearty food, at regular hours whenever possible. The more energetically you play, the more fuel you need. A good nourishing breakfast is important to start the day. A glass of juice is almost a must; one or two eggs, boiled, poached or hard-boiled; *very* little butter if you insist on a fried egg; a slice or two of *very lean* bacon (not the greasy kind some diners throw on your plate); one slice of thin whole-wheat or protein toast (I sometimes break mine right into the cup with my soft-boiled egg, thus avoiding butter entirely); a piece of cheese perhaps (don't laugh—many Europeans and Scandinavians like it for breakfast); tea, coffee or milk (preferably skimmed—it may take time, but you can learn to like it). Some people can't start the day without cereal. Okay, but don't overdo, and learn to like it with just one level teaspoon of sugar (eighteen calories only). Proteins at breakfast will tide you over to lunch time better than anything else. I'm not suggesting that you eat eggs, bacon, *and* cheese at the same meal: you should alternate on different mornings.

Luncheon should be the lightest meal of the day, especially if you have a match to play in the afternoon. Nature usually takes care of this for you, and you'll find you don't feel hungry before a match. However, you should have something, something that is easy to digest, like chicken or egg salad (not as a sandwich), or fish, or soup, or cottage cheese. Occasionally I ordered a club sandwich and ate the meat, bacon, lettuce and tomato, leaving the toast on the plate— rather messy, but usually cheaper than ordering a salad, and I was always sure of what I was getting.

At Wimbledon, in the players' lounge, where we were given free luncheons every day, the menu was always the same: fresh cold salmon (good too!); salad with cucumbers, lettuce and tomatoes; extremely thin buttered bread, light or dark; and of course tea. It all tasted fine, even though you knew exactly what was coming every day.

Dinner for tennis players ought to be the big meal of the day. You have completed your matches and need refueling for the next day. Here again you're dependent on your common sense as well as your pocketbook (or your family's). Avoid rich, starchy foods and fatty gravies. Stick to lean meat (this means trimming the fat off at times) and vegetables, salads, cheese and fruits. I don't know a single player, boy or girl, who doesn't like a good steak. In fact I have come to the conclusion that they could live on steaks forever, if they could afford them. Of course, most of them can't. Maybe it's *because* they can't that they make up for it whenever they're treated to one.

So dinner is your biggest meal, but, if you're normal, you'll get an urge for beween-meal snacks. I certainly did—so did my contemporaries—and so do my children and their friends. To help them avoid temptation, by seeing cookies and candies lying around, I try to keep apples, pears, peaches, bananas, cheese, celery and carrot sticks always available. Also hard-boiled eggs, on which I mark a big "H" with a pencil.

Mrs. Wightman had a great idea when she was running the junior tournaments at the Longwood Cricket Club: she always brought dozens of those little individual boxes of seedless raisins which she would distribute generously to all of us kids. Raisins taste sweet, they're not as caloric as candy and provide iron (only 85 calories in a small box) for energy, so I'm told. All that free giving must have cost "Mrs. Whitey" lots of dollars—but that was a fact that never entered our hungry heads in those days.

There's no need for me to tell you that too much soda pop is bad —so are thick milk shakes and ice-cream sodas. Once in a while you may pamper yourself (or let a friend treat you), but don't let it become a habit. This is the whole secret: once it becomes a habit, you are a captive and soon-to-be dead duck.

It's not just the calories you should worry about either with these drinks, although they're bad enough: it's also the cold "cold" that enters your stomach right after exercise that is bad for you. Unfortunately an ice-cold drink is the very first thing you feel like having after an hour of heated tennis in the sun, and you're so parched that you gulp down whatever it is in three seconds flat—the worst thing you can do. It doesn't even satisfy your thirst; you're ready for more right away. The best habit for you to acquire is to start with a plain glass of water, not iced, and drink it slowly. Too Spartan, you think? Not when you get used to it. Next, switch to hot tea (which quenches your thirst better than iced tea, oddly enough), with lemon or milk, and with only one or two sugar cubes (not lumps), or an artificial sweetener. After a shower and a cooling-off period, you may then allow yourself the cold drink with ice in it. Unsweetened fruit juices are fine; so is iced tea, which I always keep on hand during the summer. The low-calorie soft drinks can do you no harm and are refreshing too. But, remember, don't down any of these cold drinks too fast.

At this point there is hardly any need for me to mention that to-bacco and alcohol don't mix well with tennis or tennis players—you will have guessed my thoughts already. If you care at all about your wind, your eye and your brain, you'll keep away from these two detri-mental tempters. They can be almost as habit-forming as the wrong food. And, as with food, the sooner such a habit ensnares you, the harder for you to break away. So don't be a "show-off" (this is usu-ally the reason for starting); you can gain respect and popularity just as successfully in other less harmful ways. At least wait until you're in your twenties, when you will have a better idea of what you're doing—and of the consequences.

Extra Hints for Body Care

Don't sit around in damp clothes after playing tennis. If for some reason it's impossible to take a shower immediately, at least cover up with a sweater or jacket, or you'll find yourself with a honey of a stiff neck and sore muscles the next morning.

If you're playing in a hot, sunny climate, wear some sort of head covering—a cap, hat or visor—to protect you from sunstroke, sun-burn, dizziness, or plain old freckles and dry skin.

Use protective creams or suntan lotions if you're going to be long in the sun. This is especially advisable for girls, but it will do the boys no harm. I've seen some very red and painful noses and forearms after only two sets.

Buy sneakers that are plenty roomy, so that you can wear two pairs of socks, if you're expecting a hard game. Wear a thin pair next to your skin and a thicker pair, for cushioning, on the outside. Two pairs act as insulation and help prevent blisters under the toes and on the soles of your feet (especially on asphalt or cement courts).

If you do start getting a blister, cover it with "moleskin" or a Band-Aid. It may subside by itself, and you hope that it will. If it doesn't, sterilize a needle with the flame of a match and alcohol; insert it care-fully, not right into the bubble itself, but barely outside of it in the healthy skin, and pierce it gently from the side. In this way the liquid will be expelled through the side prick, and the bubble will be de-flated but not broken, thus leaving the injured skin intact. Healing will be faster and less sore. Put a Band-Aid on afterwards, of course, to prevent infection.

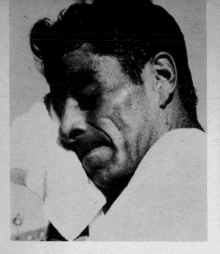

It looks as though Pancho Gonzalez suffered from the same perspiration woes as I did.

Nancy Richey Gunter knows when to cover up after a match.

You have already chosen a racket that feels comfortable in your hand, but if your racket seems to have sharp edges (and new rackets sometimes do), and you feel soreness developing where an edge is pressing, put a piece of moleskin on the sore spot as soon as possible. It sticks as well as anything and may be cut to fit any size area. At an early age, we were taught by our mother to carry moleskin, Band-Aids and safety pins with us at all times. Very good advice that you would do well to heed.

Concerning apparel: Besides choosing the style you prefer and can afford, be sure you get comfortable clothes that don't bind you anywhere, or that can keep you from reaching in any direction. You'll have enough else to think about on the court.

Concerning perspiration: This can be a serious and irritating problem. I know, because I am without a doubt the "world's champion" in this department (or was anyway). I didn't drip, I poured. There are certain things that can be done to help (nothing will cure). To keep some of the perspiration from rolling down your arm (so that you can't hold onto your racket), wear a terry-cloth sweatband for the wrist; these are available in sporting-goods stores and pro shops. There is also a nonslip spray that you can rub on the handle of the racket, as well as a sticky-grip mit-rub that also works pretty well. And if you don't mind a tan mark on your wrist, there's a specially made glove, with terry-cloth backing and leather on the inside for gripping the racket, which you can buy at specialty stores.

Also avoid drinking a cup of water every time you feel thirsty. Take a swallow if you must; better still, just swirl it around the inside of your mouth.

Obviously deodorants and nonperspirants are necessary. Try different kinds to find the one that works best for you.

Those of you who have to wear eyeglasses while playing do have a real handicap if you perspire heavily, always having to take the glasses off and wipe them. There are "no-fog" and "no-mist" products on the market that help considerably. Frankie Parker (former national champ) handled the situation as well as anyone I've seen. He would wipe his glasses quickly and competently as he was moving back into position, without apparent discomfort or delaying the game. He often wore a band around his head to keep the perspiration from dripping down his forehead into his eyes. Too much perspiring on the court may cause an excessive loss of salt in the system, which sometimes results in muscle cramps. Salt pills (sodium chloride), taken according to directions, will help prevent this situation.

Perspiration is still a nuisance, no matter how you try to cope with it. Grin and bear it; and above all don't let it keep you from playing.

10 · GAMESMANSHIP AND SPORTSMANSHIP

By now you are well on the way to being a tennis player. You have analyzed yourself and decided what sort of player you want to be; you know how to turn your disadvantages into advantages, and how to make the most of your mental and physical assets; you know quite a lot about tactics and where to place the ball; and you are supplied with a magnificent assortment of strokes.

But something is missing: you are not yet a complete tennis player. We haven't gone into the matter of your behavior on the court, whether you win or lose. Call it court manners or sportsmanship if you will. I don't like the word etiquette. There is such a narrow line to be drawn between sportsmanlike and unsportsmanlike gamesmanship that it's a tricky subject to tackle. There's an endless poker-game fascination about tennis. In no other sport, it seems to me, are the strategic possibilities so numerous, the ways to outwit your opponent so rich and varied within the accepted sportsmanlike bounds. No matter what kind of player you may be, whether you take your tennis seriously, or just play for the fun of it, you will want to win occasionally. It's not fun to lose all the time, even though it may be good exercise.

How to win at tennis without actually cheating—that is the question. And, I might add, how to do it without stepping over that thin boundary line of accepted behavior; not only according to others but according to yourself.

The standards of gamesmanship and sportsmanship vary considerably for social and tournament tennis. You can get away with little ploys in social tennis that are accepted (even respected) as fun by your opponent, who may wish he had thought of them himself. In a tournament this same bit of semitrickery would be considered unsportsmanlike. Questioning a line call is a case in point. I've seen players do this in social games who would never dream of doing it in a tournament match.

Practice Psychology

In order to be a successful gamester, you must be a kind of amateur practicing psychologist. Naturally you won't be a successful judge of others unless you have studied yourself first and you understand what your own reaction would be under the same circumstances. You will realize that your efficiency will increase or decrease as a result of anger, pleasure, annoyance, confidence, confusion, serenity, or whatever it may be. Knowing what causes you to react the way you do will help you to effect a similar reaction in your opponent, provided the circumstances are parallel, and his temperament is akin to yours. If not, you can do your best to compare his temperament with that of someone like him, whose reactions you know. Half of the fun will be in trying anyway.

Undermining Confidence

The two main links in his armor that can be made vulnerable are (1) his confidence and (2) his concentration. Let's start with confidence. The player who gets the first jump—we'll call him player A—gains a definite psychological advantage. His initial lead gives him confidence, which in turn gives him good timing and control of his shots. His opponent, player B, has got to turn the tide somehow. Obviously he must change his losing game and take chances. So let's say when player A makes a wide angle shot, pulling player B far out of court, B doesn't take the safe way and merely return the ball (after having run full speed to reach it): he shoots for a difficult winner down the line, which he just barely misses. However A realizes that the shot might just as well have been in as out, and he becomes a bit shaken and less confident. He decides not to try that particular shot again. If B had merely lobbed the ball back for an easy kill, A's confidence would have increased, and B would have tired himself for nothing. The point is that there is a science to missing the right shots, and at times it's better to take a chance and miss by a couple of inches than let your opponent make a simple put-away.

Overconfidence is another enemy of confidence. By believing his own ego, or flattery from an opponent, a player starts thinking he's better than he is. He will take reckless chances and begin to make needless errors. The result—loss of confidence. I have seen flattery used successfully in a social match. Player A tells player B that he has never seen his forehand working so well, and player B, smiling modestly, tries to hit it better and better. Naturally he falls into a string of errors, and loses face as well as confidence. This method is so obvious that it would never work in a tournament, nor would anyone try, nor would he have much time if he did try. I feel that a player so gullible as to be taken in deserves what he gets. But don't fall for it yourself.

Confidence may rise and fall like the tide, and it fluctuates so sensitively that a whole match may depend on one single point. Once confidence has left you, it's difficult, though not impossible, to recover. This is the reason why you shouldn't let things bother you and why you should try to keep a balanced perspective by holding your nerve and temper. You shouldn't feel too elated when things are going well, or too depressed when you're in a slump.

And don't brood, once the point is over, over your stupid shot or your opponent's great one. You'll lose many additional points if you do. Pull yourself together (as Arnold Palmer suggests) and think of the next point. Above all don't show your opponent you're worried: look and act confident. This is "fair" gamesmanship.

An example of unfair gamesmanship is rushing an opponent by serving before he is ready to receive. Actually he has the right to raise his hand and say, "Not ready," *without* making an attempt to hit the ball. If he makes an attempt, misses, and then says he wasn't ready, it doesn't count. But he may not know this rule or be too embarrassed to take advantage of it. Should someone try rushing you (more than a couple of times), don't hesitate to let him know that you weren't ready. In many cases it will be unintentional, due to impatience or overeagerness; you will soon be able to sense whether or not the rushing is being done on purpose.

Equally unsportsmanlike is the practice of stalling, taking too much time between points or games. This too may be purely unintentional: a person may be a slow mover, may have to wipe his eyeglasses, or may be just plain out of breath. Stalling is discourteous to an opponent if it's done often and regularly. It is bad sportsmanship if it's done on purpose. In social tennis it wouldn't matter much, since the atmosphere is casual. In fact most players probably appreciate the extra time it gives them to mop their brows or wipe the handles of their rackets. But stalling is not appreciated in tournament play.

Upsetting Concentration

Now let's turn our attention to the other possibly weak link in a player's armor: concentration. Concentration doesn't come and go as quickly as confidence, so you can regain it more easily during a match. However, you may still lose valuable points before you realize what has happened. How can you guard against losing yours? By knowing both how it can be lost and what to watch out for.

One of the easiest ways of losing it is through plain carelessness. You may have a comfortable lead of four or five games, so you unconsciously relax your guard, even start looking around to see who's playing on the next court, or who is watching on the sidelines. Before you know it, the score is tied at 5 all instead of 5-1, and you have to work your head off to pull out the set, because your opponent picked up timing and confidence during your lapse. Knowing that this can happen to *you*, you'll be prepared for its happening to your opponent and ready to take advantage of the slightest laxness on his part.

Another thing to watch out for is a foxy adversary who feigns illness or injury (perhaps unmeaningly—we'll give him the benefit of the doubt) and arrives on the court with either verbal complaints or actual bandages on a wrist, elbow or knee. Or even all three! (Don't think I'm exaggerating—this happened to me in a tournament at Easthampton one year.) Even though the injuries may be authentic, or partially authentic, don't let the situation stir your sympathy to the point of losing your concentration. Keep your mind on the game and console him or her afterwards.

Beware, also, of the exhausted foe who can hardly raise his arm to serve, who moans and groans as though he were about to collapse. Suddenly, when you think you have the match well in hand and begin to take it easy—bang!—he comes to life (phony second wind, no doubt). He rushes around retrieving your shots—and the pressure is now on *you*. Unless you're prepared for this unexpected rejuvenation, you'll have trouble getting your concentration back in time to save the match.

I hardly need mention that too much social conversation interferes with concentration. Boasting comes under the too-much-conversation category. If player A (boring anyway) starts going on about how well he did last week against so-and-so, don't be intimidated. Decide for yourself how he plays on the court. Conversely, player B (a whiner) may tell you how poorly he has been playing lately and he hopes you'll put up with his terrible game. Don't fall for this either.

As for what to watch out for in tournament matches, there are more subtle unsporting devices which players occasionally use. (Very seldom, fortunately.)

One is playing to the gallery, in order for the player to have the audience rooting for him to the distraction of his opponent. Making tragic faces at decisions; throwing points too obviously in order to seem sporting (actually you'd have to throw two points in a row to make everything come out even on a bad call); over-complimenting your opponent after he makes a good shot, when you didn't need the point anyway are all part of playing to the gallery. Fellow tournament players can see through these artifices right away, as they don't ring true. But galleries are very often fooled, not knowing the inside circumstances and not being perceptive enough to comprehend. They cheer their hero and applaud the errors of his opponent. If this ever happens to you, pretend you have earplugs in both ears, and go about your business.

Another aggravating ploy to be wary of is that of the poaching net man, the player who jumps sideways across the court to intercept his partner's shot. This applies of course to doubles. Fairly done, poaching is a fine art, *once* the ball is in play. But, if the man at the net jumps up and down *purposely* (before the ball is in play) in order to distract the eye of the player who is receiving, then it is unfair gamesmanship. Here again it's a narrow line to draw, since the poacher must be on his toes and alert to make a successful poach. It boils down to this: did he or did he not try to distract you on purpose? Try not to be distracted in any case and keep your eye on the ball rather than on the net man.

There are many people who ruin their pleasure in a sport by taking it too seriously. Don't do this to your tennis! Fortunately for all of us, tennis has a way of ironing out temperamental wrinkles and very few of them appear in the top-flight ranks. (When they do, they're often blown up out of proportion by the newspapers.) The same thing is true of the elementary rules of good sportsmanship. You may find a few dubs or weekend players who will call a ball out when it's good or who "accidentally" make a mistake in the scoring. There are mediocre golfers, too, who pick their balls out of bad lies and forget how many shots they took out of a trap. But the top-notch golfers and tennis players are keen and honest competitors who have been subjected to the discipline of the game at its best.

Here are two of the greatest players and sportsmen in tennis today. Roy Emerson of Australia carries an injured opponent, Manuel Santana of Spain, off the court during a tournament match.

Anyone who has ever played tennis at Wimbledon and Forest Hills must have a special and sentimental feeling about the lines from Kipling's "If" which are printed on a shingle just over the entrance to both center courts:

> If you can meet with triumph and disaster,
> And treat those two impostors just the same . . .

I have often wondered how many famous players from how many countries have glanced up at them. Sometimes they just flash by as you hurry past. At other times they penetrate more deeply. You are always conscious of their presence.

They suggest to me what all of us, whether or not we play in tournaments or just for fun, must learn sooner or later: fairness, sportsmanship, and fair gamesmanship.

11 · HOW TO START A TENNIS GROUP

It doesn't take a genius to be able to organize a congenial tennis group. What it does take is a little initiative and enthusiasm. You'll soon discover that you can have some of the best afternoons and summers imaginable without great effort. The reason many young people don't start organizing a group is that they don't know how, and it seems like too much effort.

I must admit that you will probably need the help of a couple of adults in the beginning (preferably an interested parent or two), who will be willing to do some of the paper work as well as the telephoning and chauffeuring. Once you get the hang of it, however, and build up a fairly competent committee of helpers, you and your friends will be able to swing it pretty much by yourselves.

You can have any size group you want, starting with four, five or six players. The larger the group, the more fun; but you'll need more than one court and more helpers to organize it if you get into the twelve-to-twenty-five bracket. Otherwise there will be too much sitting around waiting for turns.

The Round Robin

There are three good types of competition to choose from. One is called a round-robin tournament; it's probably the most popular for a one-day affair, since it gives every player a chance to play often and to play with and against all the other players. In other words it's a great mixer, like a "Paul Jones" at dances.

There are different ways of running a round robin, and you should experiment a bit to decide which method fits your particular group the best. Much depends of course on the size of your group and on whether you want to play singles or doubles.

If you have a sizable group, say fifteen or twenty, you would do well to play four games only per match. In order to figure out the number of matches to be played, multiply the number of players or teams by one less than the total number and divide by two. To simplify: if there are four players or teams, $4 \times 3 = 12$, $12 \div 2 = 6$ matches to be played. The following diagram will give you an idea

ROUND ROBIN A

4 teams — 8 players

6 MATCHES	TEAMS TO PLAY	Number of Games			
		1	2	3	4
1	Team 1 vs. Team 2				
2	Team 3 vs. Team 4				
3	Team 1 vs. Team 3				
4	Team 2 vs. Team 4				
5	Team 2 vs. Team 3				
6	Team 1 vs. Team 4				
	TOTAL GAMES				

of how this would work for four players or teams. I'll show it as for teams, which will allow for eight players. As you can see there will be six matches of four games each, and every team will have played against every other team. You'll also realize why it's helpful to have an adult around to do the paper work—especially one who is good at math. Actually, though, after each match, the players themselves can mark the number of games they won in the correct column. However, a checkup is wise, since it's so easy to put your score in the wrong column by mistake.

The team that wins the most games is the winner. In case of a tie, one or more additional matches have to be played. This adds to the excitement!

In a situation where you have an odd number of teams, you'll have to arrange things differently, since one team will have to sit out each time. Here is a diagram of an interesting schedule for five players or teams. Obviously this schedule will take more time because of the fifteen frames or matches.

Some people find that four games are too few and that there is too much hopping up and down. This is apt to be especially true with only one court and a small group of players. In this case you may want to play longer matches and decide upon the best four out of

ROUND ROBIN B

5 teams — 10 players

No. of Frames	Teams to Play		Player Sitting Out	1 Player's Name and No.	2 Player's Name and No.	3 Player's Name and No.	4 Player's Name and No.	5 Player's Name and No.
1	1 & 2	3 & 4	5					OUT
2	2 & 3	4 & 5	1	OUT				
3	3 & 4	1 & 5	2		OUT			
4	4 & 5	1 & 2	3			OUT		
5	1 & 5	2 & 3	4				OUT	
6	1 & 3	2 & 4	5					OUT
7	2 & 5	3 & 4	1	OUT				
8	3 & 5	1 & 4	2		OUT			
9	2 & 4	1 & 5	3			OUT		
10	2 & 5	1 & 3	4				OUT	
11	1 & 4	2 & 3	5					OUT
12	2 & 4	3 & 5	1	OUT				
13	1 & 3	4 & 5	2		OUT			
14	1 & 4	2 & 5	3			OUT		
15	3 & 5	1 & 2	4				OUT	

seven games—the match score may be 4-0, 4-1, 4-2, or 4-3. You should feel free to adjust the rules to best suit the occasion. Just be sure that everyone understands them.

The Tennis Ladder

Another type of stimulating competition for groups is the tennis ladder. This may continue not only all summer, but from one year to another. Here again it's a good idea to procure the aid of an adult to help you get started—then you can operate on your own. All you need is a cardboard poster with the names of all the players who want to join the group; there may be any number. Slots, with the name of one player written on each, are cut out of the placard, to be replace-

able in any position from number one to the total number of contestants.

The ladder is a challenge game. Each person is ranked on the
so-called rungs of the ladder according to his or her considered ability. The fun of this competition is to challenge someone who is rated
above you and upset him, thus displacing him on the poster and
swapping positions.

Naturally there have to be accepted rules, which may be varied
according to the circumstances (i.e., the number of players and their
ability). Ordinarily one player may challenge another player from
one to three notches above him on the ladder. If he beats him, he
changes places with him; if he loses, he stays where he is. He may not
rechallenge that player until someone else has had a go at him first.
Usually the challenge match consists of the best two out of three sets.
However, if you're a beginning group (ages twelve to fifteen years),
you may decide to play one set only.

At the end of the summer leave the ladder poster on the group
bulletin board, and you're ready to go again the next spring. It's
amazing how the ratings can change during one season. Players who
were way down in the spring may climb way up near the top by
autumn.

Of course, if you can arrange to play indoors during the winter,
so much the better. Or if you live in Florida, California, or Arizona
—lucky you—you can play all the year around, and the name slots
on your tennis ladder will get worn out by being moved so often and
will have to be replaced.

The Tournament

The third form of competition that is excellent for any group, and
certainly the best known one, is the regular tournament. The only
reason I didn't mention it first for your group is that it eliminates so
many of the players along the way. Once you're out, you're out. However, it's the climax of a season, and surely an event that every group
should plan at least once a year. Also, to avoid the prospect of half
the players being eliminated in the first round, you can have a con-
solation tournament, made up of all the contestants who were beaten
in the opening round. This can be a fine tournament in itself. At

Wimbledon, they call it "The Plate." Some very famous names have appeared on the record books as winners of The Plate—players who either had an off day, or met a top-ranking player right away, or met a player who happened to play way over his head.

Tournaments may be held in one day, or over a period of a week, or over a period of several weekends, depending on the number of players and courts and the time available.

How to Make a Tournament Draw

When the number of competitors is 4, 8, 16, 32, 64, 128, or any higher power of 2, they meet in pairs, in accordance with the system shown by the following diagram.

When the number of competitors is not a power of 2, there will be "byes" in the first round. The purpose of having these byes is to bring into the second round a number of competitors that is a power of 2. To determine the number of byes, subtract the number of competitors from the next higher power of 2; to determine the number of competitors who must play in the first round, subtract the number of byes from the total number of competitors. If the byes are even in number, one half of them are placed at the top of the draw and one half at the bottom; if they are uneven in number, there will be one more bye at the bottom than at the top. The byes in the top half shall be the names first drawn (out of a hat or a basket). The next names drawn are placed in the first round. The byes in the bottom half are drawn last.

The following diagram will show you how to make a draw with nine to sixteen competitors. It actually isn't as complicated as it sounds or looks. Once again, though, I do recommend the assistance of an adult to guide you on your way to proficiency.

Another matter you should know about in the making of a draw is the matter of "seeding." Many people ask me, "What on earth does 'seeding' mean?" It is a good rule that prevents the best players from meeting in the first round or two, the way Mrs. Molla Mallory and Suzanne Lenglen did one year at Forest Hills. The highly emotional Mlle. Lenglen came all the way from France to America to compete in our national tournament for the first and last time, only to find herself drawn against our champion Mrs. Mallory in the first round.

TOURNAMENT DRAW

To be used for 9 — 16 players
(The actual example is for 9 players)

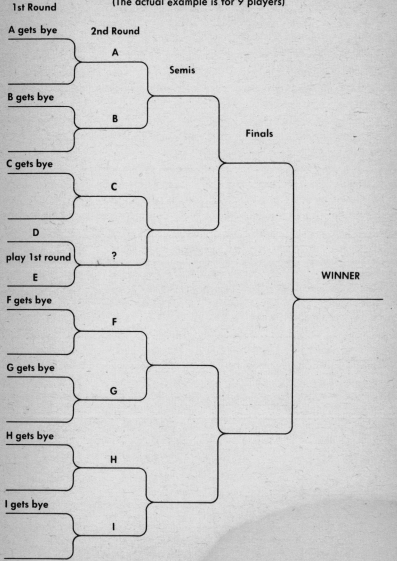

Suzanne was so upset, she almost refused to play. To make matters worse the redoubtable Molla was as hot as a firecracker. The match ended when Suzanne, nervous and unwell to begin with, defaulted and walked off the court.

This sort of thing could never happen today, because of the seeding of the top players. What it means actually is the placing of the leading contenders in a particular half, quarter, or eighth, etc., of the draw, depending on how many are entered. The rules specify that the number of seeded players shall be determined by the committee (which in your case is you and your helpers), subject to the limitation that not more than one player may be seeded for every four entries.

Let's say you're planning a tournament of eight players (small, but manageable). You may seed only two players: numbers 1 and 2 will be drawn by lot (or whatever) and should be those two whom the Committee think most likely to be the eventual finalists; the first drawn will be placed at the top of the upper half, the second at the bottom of

TOURNAMENT DRAW

for 8 players, a power of 2

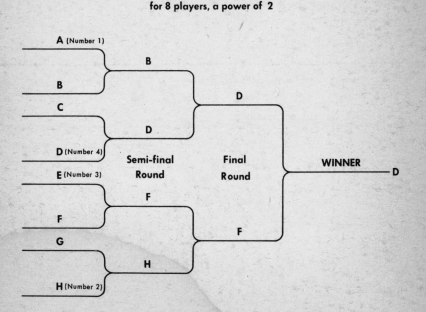

the lower half. If four are to be seeded (out of a draw of sixteen players): Numbers 1 and 2 as above. Those selected as numbers 3 and 4 are again drawn by lot; the first drawn is placed at the top of the second quarter; the second is placed at the bottom of the third quarter.

This should give you an idea. From now on you're on your own. The rest of the draw is comparatively simple: you just pull the names out of a hat and then put them down in the order they come. So if two best friends or bitter rivals meet in the first round, it's tough luck, and please don't blame me. My friend Kay Winthrop and I used to drive often from Boston to New York together to compete in the summer tournaments, and invariably we would find that we were pitted against each other in the first round. Infuriating, regrettable, but unavoidable.

For your tournament I recommend that the matches be played for the best two out of three sets (the first person to win two sets is the victor). Another suggestion is to encourage and train a few of your more intelligent friends (or their parents) to act as umpires during the matches. This will avoid a great deal of confusion and unnecessary delay when questions and problems arise. A good investment would be the purchase of the annual *U.S.L.T.A. Yearbook and Guide,* which contains loads of pertinent information.

Whichever form of competition you choose—whether it's a round robin, a tennis ladder, a tournament, or, even better, all three—you'll find that by organizing a group, or by helping to organize a group, you will open many doors, and each one will lead to a new vista.

To help you get started, there are many (seventeen, to be exact) Sectional Tennis Associations in different parts of the country, as well as nonprofit organizations, that are sponsoring tournaments and free tennis clinics (i.e., free instruction periods). They will be glad to advise you in any capacity. In the East, for instance, are the Eastern Tennis Patrons Association, with headquarters in New York City, and the Richmond Tennis Patrons Association in Richmond, Virginia. In the West (where the greatest number of United States champions have come from), there is the California Patrons Association, in Los Angeles, under the able guidance of Perry T. Jones; and farther north there is the Youth Tennis Foundation of Northern California, in San Francisco, started eight years ago by a small group of community-minded business leaders guided by James B. Moffet, known as "Mr. Tennis" in that area. They, and associations like them, are doing a great job of promoting, organizing and helping young people like you get interested in the game. They also raise funds for necessary equipment for those who don't have it, like balls and rackets and even tennis shoes. I understand that Greater Miami now has tennis instruction as a regular part of its daily physical-education class program in twenty-six junior and senior high schools.

To help you get started, there are many (seventeen, to be exact) Sectional Tennis Associations, in different parts of the country, as well as nonprofit organizations, that are sponsoring tournaments and free tennis clinics (i.e., free instruction periods). They will be glad to advise you in any capacity. In the East, for instance, are the Eastern Tennis Patrons Association, with headquarters in New York City, and the Richmond Tennis Patrons Association in Richmond, Vir-

In case you don't recognize the author, I am the second from the left, receiving congratulations from Richard Hooper after the finals of the National Senior Hard Court Tournament in Seattle, Washington, in 1968. Alphonso Smith (far left) and I won in the two tough sets over Kitty Prince and Len Dworkin. Smitty and I hadn't played together in over forty years when we won the Mass. State Juniors together.

ginia. In the West (where the greatest number of United States champions have come from), there is the California Patrons Association, in Los Angeles, and farther north there is the Youth Tennis Foundation of Northern California, in San Francisco, started eight years ago by a small group of community-minded business leaders guided by James B. Moffet, known as "Mr. Tennis" in that area. They, and associations like them, are doing a great job of promoting, organizing and helping young people like you get interested in the game. They also raise funds for necessary equipment for those who don't have it, like balls and rackets and even tennis shoes. I understand that Greater Miami now has tennis instruction as a regular part of its daily physical-education class program in twenty-six junior and senior high schools. Just within the last three years the National Junior Tennis League was formed in the east, under the spirited and able guidance of Sheridan Snyder and Ray Benton, who have built it into an exciting national organization offering underprivileged kids from all over the country a chance not only to learn tennis but to compete in tournaments. This league that started in New York City has now spread to sixteen cities and is handling 20,000 youngsters, the boys in the mornings and the girls in the afternoons. It will continue to grow.

So with all this available help from different committees and associations, you should have no trouble organizing or joining any kind of a group you wish. Go to it!

12 · A BRIEF HISTORY OF TENNIS AND A LOOK TO ITS FUTURE

Some of you may think that "tennis" is the name of the game that I'm writing about. Actually it's not—it is "lawn tennis," even though it isn't often played on lawns (or grass) anymore. In fact, grass courts are getting to be more of a luxury—and scarcer and scarcer (except in Australia and England). The reason is obvious: grass courts take a great deal of care, around-the-clock upkeep. Badly tended grass courts are much worse than uneven clay, composition or hard courts. However, a really fine grass court is so wonderful to play on, like the Centre Court at Wimbledon, Forest Hills (until and unless they're chopped up), Longwood and a few others, that tennis traditionalists as well as top players and officials are trying to keep them alive for the major international tournaments. They're doing this in spite of the growing clamor for a universal court surface which would make international competition more equitable for those countries whose players have never seen a grass court (let alone played on one), unless they have traveled abroad.

Lawn tennis is in reality the outgrowth of the old French game "Le Paume," which originated in the days of Louis IX in the thirteenth century, a game originally played in courts (or courtyards) outdoors. However, it wasn't long before the idea for indoor play met with considerable interest, so indoor courts were built to resemble the outdoor courts. About a century later the English liked what they saw in France and transported the game to their homeland, where it was called "tennis" (this game is now known in America as "court tennis").

It had its ups and downs during the next three centuries in both England and France (it suffered from charges of discrimination, cheating and gambling) and finally faded in popularity by the end of the seventeenth century.

It was in 1873 that Major Walter C. Wingfield, a British Army officer, originated the game of lawn tennis. He adapted the old classic sport of court tennis to outdoor conditions, in order to provide healthy activity at lawn parties. It caught on like wildfire and spread rapidly in England and to other countries. One of Major Wingfield's Army associates took some balls and rackets to Bermuda, where again the sport quickly caught on. In 1874 Miss Mary Outerbridge, who was visiting in Bermuda, became so interested in tennis that she brought some equipment back to the United States and introduced the new game at the Staten Island Cricket and Baseball Club in New York.

The rest is history. Tennis became extremely popular at the big social centers in the East such as Newport, Boston, Philadelphia. Interclub matches were staged and, at this point, a somewhat complicated problem presented itself: there was no standardization of rules, either here or in England. You can imagine the confusion, arguments and disagreements that must have taken place.

Obviously they did, because, after an accumulation of such arguments, a number of tennis enthusiasts decided to hold a meeting at New York's Fifth Avenue Hotel in May of 1881 (I wish I'd been there). This meeting led to agreement on a code, and to the birth of the United States Lawn Tennis Association (the U.S.L.T.A.), which has been the governing body of tennis in this country ever since. At the back of the book you'll see how the rules have grown.

The first United States National Championships were held in Newport, Rhode Island, in 1881 and remained there until 1915, when the tournament was shifted to its present location at the West Side Tennis Club in Forest Hills, New York.

Another hurdle that tennis had to overcome in its early days was its label as a "social" game, a game played only by those with plenty of money and leisure time. How could it help but be a "sissy" game? The scoring terms didn't help any either, what with a word like "love" thrown in (meaning nothing, or zero).

Maurice McLoughlin's appearance on the courts in 1912 was a special turning point: the public began to accept tennis as an exciting sport rather than merely a social pastime. "The California Comet" was a whale of an athlete with terrific energy and speed. He transformed tennis to a game of brawn as well as brains, and he developed a strong following of youngsters and young-oldsters who tried to copy his style.

On top of this he was a great sportsman with a terrific personality. One year he even hit some balls with me on a trip to Longwood after he had retired. I was ten years old. My knees were shaking so with excitement I could hardly move, but it was an occasion I'll never forget.

After McLoughlin's short but dynamic career, tennis grew by leaps and bounds. Famous names like Billy Johnston, Dick Williams and, of course, Bill Tilden came to the fore. The all-court game, with the attacking serve, the sound ground strokes and the strong net attack became the winning game, replacing the back-court style.

International tennis grew and flourished, and the world's leading players came to the United States to compete in tournaments, including the National Singles and Doubles Championships, as well as the Davis Cup matches.

The Davis Cup, as you may know, was donated by Dwight F. Davis in 1900 for the purpose of starting an annual team match between the United States and England. Now there are over fifty nations competing for this coveted trophy, which has become the symbol of tennis supremacy throughout the world.

Mrs. Wightman donated the Wightman Cup in 1923 for two teams of the top women players from the United States and Great Britain. The matches are held annually in alternate countries.

And, in 1963, the International Lawn Tennis Federation celebrated its fiftieth anniversary by initiating an international team competition for women, which is open to *all* the member nations. In the inaugural Federation Cup matches, held at the Queen's Club in London, sixteen countries were represented.

Modern tennis has come a long way since the turn of the century. Today we are in the cycle of the big serve and net attack, at the expense of ground strokes. But this will change. I've seen so many cycles. I hear people say that tennis is boring to watch nowadays— just the big serve, run up to the net, and either make or miss the volley. True, but it's nothing that a good return of serve couldn't cure. And it's not new! Anyone who saw the finals of the U.S. National Men's Singles in 1930 will recall that it was a terrific battle of the big serve and volley, with Johnny Doeg (who I believe had the finest

The surprise winner and darling of the crown at Wimbledon, England in 1971, Evonne Goolagong from Australia, leaps for a forehand volley. I bet she makes it, too.

serve I ever saw) just nosing out Frank Shields (people forget what a powerful serve he had, too) 16-14 in the fourth set. Neither of these two young men had much in the way of ground strokes, but what a job it was to break through their serves. It took players like Fred Perry and Don Budge, with their great returns of serve, to do this. All it would take would be another Budge or Gonzalez to beat the Lavers and Smiths of today.

There are more good young players in all countries today than there ever have been in the history of the sport. And from these youngsters will rise the champions of the future. Two such champions have already appeared, not fictional figures on the horizon but living, colorful girls, both entirely different but enchanting in their own way. It happened in 1971.

The first to reach prominence was Evonne (pronounced Avon) Goolagong, a nineteen year old charmer from Australia. Like the proverbial "breath of fresh air" she came from the out-break town of Barellan, a sheep-raising settlement about four-hundred miles south-west of Sydney.

To the delight and surprise of the entire tennis world, Evonne won the 1971 French and then Wimbledon Singles Championship, beating former three-time Wimbledon Champ, Margaret Smith Court in the finals in straight sets 6-4, 6-1, having beaten another three-time champion, Billie Jean King in the semi-finals 6-4, 6-4. Quite a feat. It had been well known that this talented, imaginative youngster would one day become a leading star (although it is always difficult to predict for sure), but no-one thought that it would happen so soon. Even her teacher and adopted father, Vic Edwards, who had coached her from the age of eleven, thought it would take another couple of years before she would be no. 1.

Her early life was fascinating and unbelievable for a future champion. How could one have imagined that the third child of a part aboriginal father and mother would ever be given the opportunity of competing with the world's best in any field, let alone tennis, one of the most sophisticated sports of all, combining perhaps the most physical and mental qualities of any other game.

How did it happen? What did she have?

It started to happen when Evonne was discovered on Barellan's one tennis court by visiting tennis buffs from Sydney, when she was about nine or ten years old. She was soon brought to the big city by Vic Edwards, the head of the largest tennis school in Australia, who recognized her great potential. She had extraordinary timing and coordination even then. Edwards persuaded her father and mother to let Evonne live with him and his wife, and when she was fourteen she became a legally adopted member of the Edwards family, although she kept her own family name of Goolagong. (What a marvelous name—its literal translation means "nose of a kangaroo".)

Her improvement from then on was rapid and exciting, and even though she managed to finish high school and a secretarial course, her main life was devoted to tennis. She was determined to be the best.

I watched her Wimbledon finals against Margaret Court on our little portable TV set in a cabin on a lake just south of Pawling, N. Y. I had never seen her play before, although I had read a great deal about her in the sports pages. The qualities that struck me the most were her amazing anticipation, her grace and mobility in covering court, her uncanny selection of shots (strategy in other words), and last but not least, her seeming enjoyment of the game. So many of today's young tournament players look so grim and unhappy that you wonder why they enter tournaments if they don't enjoy them. Concentration is one thing; but sadness is another. Not so with Evonne —she is bubbly and enthusiastic, without letting doubtful decisions disturb either her or her concentration. Very refreshing.

Equally refreshing in a completely different way, was the second champion to arrive on the national tennis scene in 1971, a slim, attractive sixteen year old girl from Fort Lauderdale, Florida, named

Chris Evert of Fort Lauderdale, Fla., the 16-year-old sensation of the 1971 U.S. Open Championships at Forest Hills, is shown here with her strongest weapon, her two-handed backhand. Notice her concentration.

Chris Evert. I had known her father, Jimmy Evert, quite a few years ago when I was in my prime. He was a fine player in his own right. But who would have guessed then that he would have a daughter, Chrissy, who was to become the heroine of Forest Hills who saved the U.S. Open Championships from financial disaster when the top men players decided not to play. It was due to Chris's courage, her magnetism and extraordinary tennis ability, especially for one so young, that drew the crowds to the stadium. Every day she played there was a huge, enthusiastic gallery, and tournament director, Vic Seixas, wisely scheduled her on the center court each time, where she made an astonishing string of upsets until she was finally downed in the semi's by an unflappable Billie Jean King 6-3, 6-2, who went on to win the championship.

Chris Evert, who is the second of four children, started to play tennis at the age of five and has been playing about five hours a day ever since. Having been brought up on slow clay courts, her ground strokes are sound and consistent, her best shot being her two-handed backhand which is well disguised and accurate. She can practically thread a needle with it. Her serve and volley need to be improved, and she knows this. But it is her extraordinary temperament that impressed me the most, watching her play at Forest Hills in '71. We had all heard that she was worth watching when the word got around that she had won over 40 straight matches without a loss since February and that she had had an outstanding win in the Wightman Cup matches in Cleveland in August against Virginia Wade in the fifth and deciding singles. Carole Graebner, the U.S. Wightman Cup Captain, told me on her return to N. Y. that she was so impressed by Chris's play, that she thought Chris would surprise everyone at Forest Hills. However, we weren't prepared for what we saw. She doesn't impress you all at once; she looks like another talented youngster with lovely groundstrokes. But the more you watch, the more you notice her unusual qualities. She has the poise and concentration of a Helen Wills, as well as the determination and steadiness of a Maureen Connolly. She also responds to pressure with astonishing calm and maturity as was proved in her match against Mary Ann Eisel in the second round of the U.S. Open. She was down six match points and won. Quite a competitor—and quite a girl.

Everyone now wonders how Chrissy and Evonne would come out against each other. On paper Evonne seems to have a definite ·edge in international experience. But you can't be sure. Anyway it should be something to see.

13. "Open Tennis and Women's Lob"

With the long-awaited advent of Open Tennis in 1968, many people assumed and hoped that tennis at last would come into its own and reach, if not pass, golf in popularity and public acceptance. It started out that way too. People flocked to the big tournaments as never before, and players were getting large amounts of money "over the table" for a change. Everything seemed serene and hopes were high.

But optimism was premature. Troubles began. The smell of money and the desire for power entered the picture. Different factions began to jockey for position, each vying for a certain amount of control.

There was the staid and traditional International Lawn Tennis Federation (I.L.T.F.), which is made up of 93 National Associations, including of course our United States Lawn Tennis Association (U.S.L.T.A.). These well meaning associations were sincerely trying to be broadminded about the whole thing, but they actually didn't want to let go of their hold of the purse strings or the direction of future tennis. They were afraid of this new commercialism that had reared its head and which they felt might be harmful to junior players. They really wanted to keep the game the way it had been for the last few decades, without realizing that times had changed so much that tennis simply couldn't stay the same any longer.

Another major faction in tennis troubles today is the World Champion Tennis Group (W.C.T.), headed by Texas millionaire Lamar Hunt, assisted by his executive director, Englishman Mike Davies. W.C.T. has 32 of the top tennis professionals in the world, including Rod Laver, John Newcombe, Arthur Ashe, Ken Rosewall, Tom Okker, etc. These are the contract pros. They're under contract to W.C.T., which gives them an annual guarantee plus airplane traveling expenses. In return they must play when and where they are told. But they are well taken care of, and all are making more money than they ever dreamed of. The leader, Rod Laver, cleared over $240,000 in 1971. In fact Rod became the first tennis millionaire in November 1971, even though he lost the final match in Dallas,

Still another great Australian player is John Newcombe, the 1967 and 1971 Wimbledon Champion and 1967 U.S. Champion. With his excellent all-around game and athletic ability, handsome John is able to beat anyone on a given day and may continue to do so for some time to come.

Texas to Ken Rosewall 6-4, 1-6, 7-6, 7-6. I loved the New York Times headlines the day after the match "Laver has to settle for a million." The report also said that Laver played in a gold outfit from shirt to socks. Ken Rosewall was wearing blue. Maybe color is here to stay. Not to mention the fact that it televises better.

Then there are the independent pros, who can play open tournaments and earn prize money, but are not under contract. Oddly enough the independent pros are allowed to play on the Davis Cup Team, whereas the contract pros are not. This situation will no doubt be straightened out eventually. They can make their own schedules. Players like Cliff Richey and Clark Graebner, for instance, do very well as independents. Stan Smith, the Davis Cup star who had a wonderful win in the 1971 U.S. Open, will be able to call his own shots when he gets out of the army.

Now we come to the women players and the rebellion that started the Women's Pro Tour—"Women's Lob" as it came to be called. I had heard mutterings during the summer of 1970 that the girls weren't too happy about the big difference in prize money being offered the men and women. But matters came to a head at Forest Hills that year where I attended a press conference the girls had called underneath the stadium. The thing that had burst the balloon was the prize money ratio for the upcoming Pacific South West Open Tournament in Los Angeles to be held in a couple of weeks. The purse for the women was to be less than one-eighth of that for the men. Ordinarily the ratio was about five-to-one, or at Forest Hills, three-to-one, and in Europe, two-and-a-half-to-one. But less than eight-to-one! Unthinkable. Hence the meeting and what to do about it. Billie Jean King and Rosemary Casals had a talk with Gladys Heldman, the editor and publisher of World Tennis magazine, and asked for her help. She tried to persuade Jack Kramer, the tournament director of the Pacific South West, to raise the purse for the women, but he remained adamant. So Gladys went into quick action and arranged for another tournament that same week to be held in Houston, Texas, where she had a home. With lots of last-minute help from the local tennis committees and friends, who sold hundreds of tickets, plus an enthusiastic sponsor, Virginia Slims cigarettes, who

The master, Ken Rosewall, of Australia, reaching for a wide forehand with his favorite aluminum racket during his great win over Rod Laver in the final match of the first "World Championship of Tennis" in Dallas, Texas. Just for the record, Ken picked up a tidy $50,000 for his afternoon's work, raising his season's earnings to $136,000. Not bad for a 5-foot-7-inch 37-year-old veteran.

The first tennis millionaire in the history of the game, "The Rocket," Rod Laver, from Australia (now living in California with his wife and son), is about to hit a shoulder-high backhand. Rod also has the distinction of having won the Grand Slam twice!

Stan Smith of Pasadena, California, had his greatest season in 1971. This tall, popular champion won the men's singles of the U.S. Open Championships in 1971 and reached the finals at Wimbledon. Stan has also been a mainstay on our U.S. Davis Cup Team, having won all his matches when the chips were down.

naturally wanted the girls to come "a Long Way" the tournament was a success. It was able to offer the girls $7500 in prize money. The original eight girls who played become contract pros to World Tennis for one dollar a year. Even the first round losers received $300, enough for expense money. Women's Lob was on its way.

Since then many more have joined the World Tennis Women's Pro tour, and there are now fifty-one girls included on the active list representing twelve countries. Besides Billie Jean King, other outstanding stars are Francoise Durr (No. 1 in France), Helga Niessen Mastoff (No. 1 in Germany) Virginia Wade (No. 1 in Great Britain), Betty Stove (No. 1 in The Netherlands), Kerry Melville and Judy Dalton of Australia (both on the world's first ten), Julie Heldman (she won two of her four matches against Evonne Goolagong in the 1971 Dewar Cup circuit in England), Rose Casals (runner-up at Forest Hills in 1971 and No. 4 in the world), and Nancy Richey Gunter (three times No. 1 in the U.S.).

Other notables on the tour are Helen Gourlay and Karen Krantzcke of Australia, Maria Nasuelli of Italy, Lita Liem and Lany Kaligis from Indonesia, Marie Neumannova from Czechoslovakia, Jane O'Hara and Vicki Berner from Canada, Madeleine Pegel from Sweden, U.S. Wightman Cuppers Mary Ann Eisel, Valerie Ziegenfuss and Kristie Pigeon, U.S. Amateur Champ Eliza Pande, and four time American Tennis Association Champion Bonnie Logan.

It is exciting to think that any of these girls has a chance to reach the top in the coming years and upset some of the present champions of today.

In the winter of 1971 Gladys Heldman was able to set up a whole new circuit for the girls, with the help of Virginia Slims. From January to May they played in thirteen tournaments with prize money of between ten and twelve thousand dollars with a thirty thousand dollar tournament in Las Vegas. Imagine! Wherever possible, local corporations footed the bill and acted as sponsors. Wherever not, Virginia Slims was ready and willing to put up the necessary money.

Naturally the women players were happy. They had never earned so much money. By May of 1971, four players, Billie Jean King, Ann Jones, Rosemary Casals and Francoise Durr had each earned over

Some of the Women's Pro Tour members posing at Forest Hills on their new court-surface.

twenty-five thousand dollars apiece. And in October of that year, Billie Jean, by winning the Virginia Slims Thunderbird tournament in Phoenix, Arizona, became the first female athlete in history to earn more than one-hundred thousand dollars in a year in competition sports. She even received a personal phone call from President Nixon congratulating her. In 1972 the average prize money for each winter tournament has been advanced to $20,850 as compared to $12,000 in 1971.

Now that I have discussed the four most involved groups of modern tournament tennis, the I.L.T.F., W.C.T., the Independent Pros, and the Women Pros, with players happier and making more money than ever before, you may rightfully wonder how there could be serious tennis troubles. Well, believe me, there are. Things have reached such a stage that the I.L.T.F. and our U.S.L.T.A. have threatened to disallow the W.C.T. players and the Women's Pro group from competing in any sanctioned tournaments. This would include of course Wimbledon and Forest Hills, where the big name players made their reputations in the first place. It would mean that the contract pros could only play in arenas or unsanctioned tournaments. It would also mean that the big tournaments in our country, most especially Forest Hills, would go back to smaller crowds, the independent pros and amateurs. But the public wants to see the best.

How did the situation come about, and why can't the management of two big, supposedly intelligent groups, the I.L.T.F. and W.C.T., get along together. Apparently each group thinks that the other is trying to push it around. The I.L.T.F. thinks that Lamar Hunt is an intruder, encroaching on their property, whereas Hunt, an altruistic businessman, who wants to help build tennis into a prosperous worldwide sport, is finding it much more difficult than he thought to get along with an organization that has been in control for so many years.

In 1971, W.C.T. organized a million-dollar tournament tour; the I.L.T.F. ran a million-and-a-half dollar circuit itself. Two competing tours. There was bound to be rivalry. Both groups recognized the problem and scheduled meetings to smooth the troubled waters. Unfortunately these meetings proved fruitless. Neither side would bend enough. W.C.T. knew it controlled the top players, and the I.L.T.F. knew it controlled the prestigious tournaments and that there would be other players coming up to replace the Rosewalls and Ashes of today.

The scheduling of the tournaments obviously had a lot to do with the breakdown of the negotiations. Also there were the matters of television contracts, the types of court surfaces, the scoring rules and the choice of tennis balls that added to the complications. More meetings are scheduled, and maybe by the time you read this book, matters will have been resolved. Maybe the U.S.L.T.A. will have broken away from the I.L.T.F. and be standing on its own feet. Who knows. Be that as it may, tennis is a sport that will outlive any organizations.

14. Sudden Death—The New Tie Breaker

Nothing intrigued the spectators more in 1970 (besides the actual tennis of course) than the innovation of "Sudden Death", the best-of-nine points tie-breaker system, invented by Jimmy Van Alen of Newport, R.I. There is also a 12 point tie-breaker which some prefer. It was used experimentally in 1970 in the U.S. Open Championships by Tournament Director Bill Talbert, and given the official okay by astute Tournament Chairman Joseph Cullman, the dual purpose being to add to the excitement of the matches and maybe more important, to help with the scheduling of the daily matches in order to avoid some of those long drawn out men's five set encounters that can drag on for hours.

It was such a dramatic success in 1970 that it was approved permanently by the I.L.T.F. and the U.S.L.T.A. in 1971.

Basically, this is how Sudden Death works. When the score of a set gets to be six games all, the nine point system starts, the first one to get five points being the winner. The player who would ordinarily be serving next, serves the first two points (points 1 and 2) starting from the right court and then from the left. The opposing player, who would have served next, serves the following two points (points 3 and 4), also from the right and then left court. Then they change sides, and the first player again serves twice (points 5 and 6) if necessary—he may have won five straight points, in which case the set is over. If not, the opposing player then may serve the three remaining points, if necessary. Very often sets have been decided by that final ninth point, after each player has won four points apiece. The suspense builds up. You can imagine the dramatic possibilities of this final "moment of truth"—one point to determine an entire set. Bill Talbert again got an idea. In 1971, when he was both Tournament Director and Chairman, he added an innovation of his own: red signal flags to alert the spectators. Whenever a set score reached six all in games, red flags were hoisted on the side of the umpire's chair, and people rushed to see the excitement.

Maybe the red flags will remain, maybe they won't. But it seems certain that some variety of the tie-breaker Sudden Death system is destined to stay, whether it's 9 points or 12 points, especially if television gets seriously involved in tennis when time scheduling is of the utmost importance.

There were those who swore by it. They said it gave them added zip to their serves and volleys, more power on ground strokes with less effort; they insisted that it cured (or at least eased) the pain of a tennis elbow. They did admit though, that it took some adjusting to get used to it.

Then there were the traditionalists who were reluctant to switch from wood although they condescendingly gave steel a try in the beginning. Some of them actually did switch. The ones who refused, claimed that it didn't feel or look or sound like a real tennis racket at all. On top of which they said the middle of the racket (the sweet hitting-spot) was in a different place due to the rounder shape, and that if you didn't hit the ball exactly on center, you were lost. (Racket manufacturers deny this.) They also argued that a delicate "drop volley" didn't drop properly—there wasn't the same "touch". Some even resented the fact that when they accidently hit a ball "on the wood", it was on steel instead. (I can sympathize here—some of my most successful shots have been hit off the wood.)

Obviously in the beginning there were considerable differences of opinion. But human nature being what it is, there were plenty of tennis players like me who wanted to own both or either. I have seven rackets myself, both wood and metal, and I take turns, depending on the mood I'm in or how strong I feel.

Since the initial flurry about the steel racket, there have been other metals and fiberglas used by the manufacturers, and different combinations tried out by various sporting goods companies. The aluminum racket has proved to be very popular with tournament players. In fact Ken Rosewall won the 1971 W.C.T. finals in Dallas, Texas, using his new aluminum racket. There are also wooden rackets, reinforced by steel or fiberglas, that are selling well and that last for a long time. But, surprisingly, the price of wooden rackets is going up, due to the shortage of the good wood that rackets are made of, especially ash. So, whereas people thought steel was the expensive racket in 1967, now it seems that a top quality wooden one will retain its former high status symbol. Besides which some of the metal rackets are not as strong as originally predicted, and there have been reports of breakage.

Besides the successful tennis racket business, tennis balls are selling at a terrific rate. Not only the white balls with varying degrees of hardness and surface nap for different types of courts, but also a surprisingly popular yellow (very good for indoor play and late-afternoon fading light), plus (believe it or not) fuschia (!). The court surface makers and installers are thriving. Over the years they have experimented with all sorts of materials to suit all purposes and pocketbooks. The list is narrowing down to the successful ones that have withstood the test of time and harsh treatment, indoors and out, under tough conditions.

And so it goes in the tennis world for the moment. Everytime I look out of an office building in N. Y. and see a flat-top, I think, "Why can't they build a tennis court there?" Why not indeed, with a bubble on top for year 'round play. There would then be almost enought courts for everybody. No, I take that back—there will never be quite enough tennis courts for everyone who would like to play. However, it's enough for us to know that tennis will remain, under whatever conditions it is played, the finest game there is for us, for our children, and our children's children.

15. The Tennis Boom

The Tennis Boom is on. More people are playing tennis today than ever before. Tennis business is growing in leaps and bounds. A survey taken for the U.S.L.T.A. in May of 1971 by Arthur Nielsen, the television rating man, also a tennis buff, showed that tennis was right on the heels of golf, as to the number of players, with 10.6 million tennis players vs. golf's claim of 12 million. This same survey also knocked down a popular concept that tennis was mostly for young people. It seems that 3.2 times more adults than teenagers play. Here were the figures:

Men 3,860,000
Women 3,620,000
Teenagers 2,350,000
Children 835,000

Very surprising and interesting figures.

The growth of courts and clubs is also interesting. Outdoor clubs are growing at an unprecedented rated. Tennis condominiums are springing up all over the country. Cities that had only a small and steady amount of tennis activity ten years ago are now experiencing extraordinary growth.

The development of indoor courts and facilities is perhaps just as spectactular as the outdoor. Fifteen years ago there were fewer than fifty indoor clubs in the country. During the next five years three hundred more clubs had been built. In another five years the number increased to seven hundred. Now it is well past twelve hundred. Since each indoor facility costs a minimum of $250,000 depending on the number of courts, this is truly amazing. And from what I can determine they're all making money and people are lining up to join.

Tennis camps are sprouting up all over the place in this country and abroad, many of them being run by former or present champions who use their vast experience and reputations to attract customers of all ages. Don Budge, Pancho Gonzales, John Newcombe, Gardnar Mulloy, to name a few famous ones, are doing an outstanding job of running successful camps. Harry Hopman, the former highly suc-

154

cessful Australian Davis Cup captain, is another who has a long
waiting list at his tennis camps. They are not just for juniors either.
Harry's session for adults at Amherst College in the summertime is
a complete sellout. Adult tennis camps are the new rage. However,
for a refreshing switch, in Long Island where Hopman helps businessman Hy Zausner run the Port Washington Tennis Academy, they
have made a rule that no adults be allowed on the courts after 1:00
P.M. on Saturdays nor after 3:00 P.M. on Sundays. They figure that
grownups can afford their own clubs.

Tennis manufacturers are reporting great business with rackets,
balls and nets etc. As was predicted earlier, the battle between the
metal and wood racket has subsided. People are buying both. In the
beginning the advent of the steel racket made such a stir that everyone thought it would revolutionize the entire racket industry. What
had started this frenzied wave of interest, this publicity agent's
dream? Actually, it started during the 1967 U.S. National Championships at Forest Hills, N. Y., when three high-ranking U.S. players
played better than ever before. Californian Billie Jean King won the
women's singles for the first time and gave the steel racket much of
the credit. (I feel sure she would have won it anyway.) Clark Graebner, from Cleveland, Ohio, got to the men's finals for the first time
and also paid honor to the new steel racket. So did Manhattan law-
yer, Gene Scott, a week-end player, who surprised everyone, including himself, by reaching the semi-finals.

Naturally after the great success of these three players and the
ensuing publicity about the steel racket in national magazines and
newspapers, the public sat up and took notice. Not only did people
take notice but they couldn't resist buying and trying for themselves.
It was the "In" thing to do. So buy they did, to such a degree that
sporting goods companies had trouble keeping up with the demand.
The question now was, would the fad last, or was the steel racket
merely a flash in the pan?

RULES OF LAWN TENNIS
AND
CASES AND DECISIONS

Explanatory Note

The appended Code of Rules, and Cases and Decisions, revised to 1959 is the Official Code of the International Lawn Tennis Federation, of which the United States Lawn Tennis Association is a member.

Italicized Explanations, while not official utterances, may be considered a correct guide for interpreting the Rules. They have been prepared by the Tennis Umpires Association to amplify and explain the formal Code.

THE SINGLES GAME
Rule 1

Dimensions and Equipment

The Court shall be a rectangle, 78 feet long and 27 feet wide. It shall be divided across the middle by a net, suspended from a cord or metal cable of a maximum diameter of one-third of an inch, the ends of which shall be attached to, or pass over, the tops of two posts, 3 feet 6 inches high, the center of which shall be 3 feet outside the Court on each side. The height of the net shall be 3 feet at the center, where it shall be held down taut by a strap not more than 2 inches wide. There shall be a band covering the cord or metal cable and the top of the net not less than 2 inches nor more than 2½ inches in depth on each side. The lines bounding the ends and sides of the Court shall respectively be called the Base-lines and the Side-lines. On each side of the net, at a distance of 21 feet from it and parallel with it, shall be drawn the Service-lines. The space on each side of the net between the service-line and the side-lines shall be divided into two equal parts called the service-courts by the center service-line, which must be 2 inches in width, drawn half-way between, and parallel with, the side-lines. Each base-line shall be bisected by an imaginary continuation of the center service-line to a line 4 inches in length and 2 inches in width called the center mark drawn inside the Court, at right angles to and in contact with such base-lines. All other lines shall not be less than 1 inch nor more than 2 inches in width, except the base-line, which may be 4 inches in width, and all measurements shall be made to the outside of the lines.

Note—In the case of the International Lawn Tennis Championship (Davis Cup) or other Official Championships of the International Federation, there shall be a space behind each base-line of not less than 21 feet and at the sides of not less than 12 feet.

Explanation of Rule 1

The posts in doubles should be 3 feet outside the doubles court.

The net should be 33 feet wide for a singles court, and 42 feet wide for a doubles court. It should touch the ground along its entire length and come flush to the posts at all points.

It is well to have a stick 3 feet, 6 inches long, with a notch cut in at the 3-foot mark, for the purpose of measuring the height of the net at the posts and in the center. These measurements, as well as the measurements of the court itself, always should be made before starting to play an important match.

DIAGRAM AND DIMENSIONS OF TENNIS COURT
Rule 2

Permanent Fixtures

The permanent fixtures of the Court shall include not only the net, posts, cord or metal cable, strap and band, but also, where there are any such, the back and side stops, the stands, fixed or movable seats and chairs round the Court, and their occupants, all other fixtures around and above the Court, and the umpire, Foot-fault Judge and Linesmen when in their respective places.

Note—For the purpose of this Rule, the word "Umpire" comprehends the umpire and all those persons designated to assist him in the conduct of a match.

Rule 3

Ball—Size, Weight and Bound

The ball shall have a uniform outer surface. If there are any seams they shall be stitchless. The ball shall be more than two and a half inches and less than two and five-eighths inches in diameter, and more than two ounces and less than two and one-sixteenth ounces in weight. The ball shall have a bound of more than 53 inches and less than 58 inches when dropped 100 inches upon a concrete base, and a deformation of more than .265 of an inch and less than .290 of an inch when subjected to a pressure of 18 lb. applied to each end of any diameter. All tests for bound, size and deformation shall be made in accordance with the Regulations in the Appendix hereto.

"How often may the player have new balls?"

According to Tournament Regulation 14 (g) the Umpire, subject to the approval of the Referee, may decide when new balls are required to insure fairness of playing conditions. In matches where there is no Umpire, the players should agree beforehand on this matter.

Rule 4

Server and Receiver

The Players shall stand on opposite sides of the net; the player who first delivers the ball shall be called the Server, and the other the Receiver.

Case 1. Does a player, attempting a stroke, lose the point if he crosses an imaginary line in the extension of the net, (a) before striking the ball (b) after striking the ball?

Decision. He does not lose the point in either case by crossing the imaginary line, and provided he does not enter the lines bounding his opponent's court. (Rule 18(e)). In regard to hindrance, his opponent may ask for the decision of the umpire under Rules 19 and 23.

Case 2. The Server claims that the Receiver must stand within the limits bounding his court. Is this necessary?

Decision. No. The Receiver may stand wherever he pleases on his own side of the net.

Rule 5

Choice of Sides and Service

The choice of sides and the right to be Server or Receiver in the first game shall be decided by toss. The player winning the toss may choose or require his opponent to choose;

(a) The right to be Server or Receiver, in which case the other player shall choose the side; or

(b) The side, in which case the other player shall choose the right to be Server or Receiver.

Rule 6

Delivery of Service

The service shall be delivered in the following manner. Immediately before commencing to serve, the Server shall stand with both feet at rest behind (i.e., farther from the net than) the base-line, and within the imaginary continuations of the center-mark and side-line. The Server shall then project the ball by hand into the air in any direction and before it hits the ground strike it with his racket, and the delivery shall be deemed to have been completed at the moment of the impact of the racket and the ball. A player with the use of only one arm may utilize his racket for the projection.

Case 1. May the Server in a singles game take his stand behind the portion of the base-line between the side-lines of the singles court and the doubles court?

Decision. No.

Case 2. If a player, when serving, throws up two or more balls instead of one, does he lose that service?

Decision. No. A let should be called, but if the umpire regards the action as deliberate he may take action under Rule 19.

Case 3. If a ball in play becomes broken, should a let be called?

Decision. Yes.

Case 4. May a player serve underhand?

Decision. Yes. There is no restriction regarding the kind of service which may be used; that is, the player may use an underhand or overhand service at his discretion.

Rule 7

Foot Fault

The Server shall throughout the delivery of the service:

(a) Not change his position by walking or running.

(b) Not touch, with either foot, any area other than that behind the base-line within the imaginary extension of the center-mark and side-line.

Note.—The following interpretation of Rule 7 was approved by the International Federation on 9th July 1958:—

(a) The Server shall not, by slight movements of the feet which do not materially affect the location originally taken up by him, be deemed "to change his position by walking or running."

(b) The word "foot" means the extremity of the leg below the ankle.

Rule 8

From Alternate Courts

(a) In delivering the service, the Server shall stand alternately behind the right and left Courts, beginning from the right in every game. If service from a wrong half of the Court occurs and is undetected, all play resulting from such wrong service or services shall stand, but the inaccuracy of the station shall be corrected immediately if it is discovered.

(b) The ball served shall pass over the net and hit the ground within the Service Court which is diagonally opposite, or upon any line bounding such Court, before the Receiver returns it.

Explanation of Rule 8

In the absence of a Linesman and Umpire, it is customary for the Receiver to determine whether the service is good or not.

Rule 9

Faults

The Service is a fault:

(a) If the Server commit any breach of Rules 6, 7 or 8;

(b) If he miss the ball in attempting to strike it;

(c) If the ball served touch a permanent fixture (other than the net, strap or band) before it hits the ground.

Case 1. After throwing a ball up preparatory to serving, the Server decides not to strike at it and catches it instead. Is it a fault?

Decision. No.

Case 2. In serving in a singles game played on a doubles court with doubles and singles net posts, the ball hits a singles post and then hits the ground within the lines of the correct service court. Is this a fault or a let?

Decision. In serving it is a fault, because the singles post, the doubles post, and that portion of the net, strap or band between them are permanent fixtures. (Rules 2 and 9, and note to Rule 22.)

Rule 10

Service After a Fault

After a fault (if it be the first fault) the Server shall serve again from behind the same half of the court from which he served that fault, unless the service was from the wrong half, when, in accordance with Rule 8, the Server shall be entitled to one service only from behind the other half. A fault may not be claimed after the next service has been delivered.

Case 1. A player serves from a wrong court. He loses the point and then claims it was a fault because of his wrong station.

Decision. The point stands as played and the next service should be from the correct station according to the score.

Case 2. The point score being 15 all, the Server, by mistake, serves from the left court. He wins the point. He then serves again from the right hand court, delivering a fault. The mistake in station is then discovered. Is he entitled to the previous point? From which court should he next serve?

Decision. The previous point stands. The next service should be from the left court, the score being 30/15, and the Server has served one fault.

Rule 11

Receiver Must Be Ready

The Server shall not serve until the Receiver is ready. If the latter attempt to return the service, he shall be deemed ready. If, however, the Receiver signify that he is not ready, he may not claim a fault because the ball does not hit the ground within the limits fixed for the service.

Explanation of Rule 11

The Server must wait until the Receiver is ready for the second service as well as the first, and if the Receiver claims to be not ready and does not make any effort to return a service, the Server may not claim the point, even though the service was good.

Rule 12

A Let

In all cases where a let has to be called under the rules, or to provide for an interruption to play, it shall have the following interpretation:

(a) When called solely in respect of a service, that one service only shall be re-played.

(b) When called under any other circumstance, the point shall be re-played.

Case 1. A service is interrupted by some cause outside those defined in Rule 13. Should the service only be re-played?

Decision. No, the whole point must be re-played.

Rule 13

The service is a let:

(a) If the ball served touch the net, strap or band, and is otherwise good, or, after touching the net, strap or band, touch the Receiver or anything which he wears or carries before hitting the ground.

(b) If a service or a fault be delivered when the Receiver is not ready (see Rule 11). In case of a let, that particular service shall not count, and the Server shall serve again, but a service let does not annul a previous fault.

Rule 14

When Receiver Becomes Server

At the end of the first game the Receiver shall become the Server, and the Server Receiver; and so on alternately in all the subsequent games of a match. If a player serve out of turn, the player who ought to have served shall serve as soon as the mistake is discovered, but all points scored before such discovery shall be reckoned. If a game shall have been completed before such discovery, the order of service remains as altered. A fault served before such discovery shall not be reckoned.

Rule 15

Ball in Play Till Point Decided

A ball is in play from the moment at which it is delivered in service. Unless a fault or a let be called, it remains in play until the point is decided.

Case 1. A ball is played into the net; the player on the other side, thinking that the ball is coming over, strikes at it and hits the net. Who loses the point?

Decision. If the player touched the net while the ball was still in play, he loses the point.

Rule 16

Server Wins Point

The Server wins the point:

(a) If the ball served, not being a let under Rule 13, touch the Receiver or anything which he wears or carries, before it hits the ground.

(b) If the Receiver otherwise lose the point as provided by Rule 18.

Rule 17

Receiver Wins Point

The Receiver wins the point:

(a) If the Server serve two consecutive faults;

(b) If the Server otherwise lose the point as provided by Rule 18.

Rule 18

Player Loses Point

A player loses the point if:

(a) He fail, before the ball in play has hit the ground twice consecutively to return it directly over the net (except as provided in Rule 22(a) or (c)); or

(b) He return the ball in play so that it hits the ground, a permanent fixture, or other object, outside any of the lines which bound his opponent's Court (except as provided in Rule 22(a) and (c)); or

(c) He volley the ball and fail to make a good return even when standing outside the Court; or

(d) He touch or strike the ball in play with his racket more than once in making a stroke; or

(e) He or his racket (in his hand or otherwise) or anything which he wears or carries touch the net, posts, cord or metal cable, strap or band, or the ground within his opponent's Court at any time while the ball is in play; or

(f) He volley the ball before it has passed the net; or

(g) The ball in play touch him or anything that he wears or carries, except his racket in his hand or hands; or

(h) He throws his racket at and hits the ball.

Case 1. In delivering a first service which falls outside the proper court, the Server's racket slips out of his hand and flies into the net. Does he lose the point?

Decision. If his racket touches the net whilst the ball is in play, the Server loses the point. (Rule 18(e).)

Case 2. In serving, the racket flies from the Server's hand and touches the net before the ball has touched the ground. Is this a fault, or does the player lose the point?

Decision. The Server loses the point because his racket touches the net whilst the ball is in play. (Rule 18(e).)

Case 3. A and B are playing against C and D. A is serving to D. C touches the net before the ball touches the ground. A fault is then called because the service falls outside the service court. Do C and D lose the point?

Decision. The call "fault" is an erroneous one. C and D have already lost the point before "fault" could be called, because C touched the net whilst the ball was in play. (Rule 18(e).)

Case 4. May a player jump over the net into his opponent's court while the ball is in play and not suffer penalty?

Decision. No; he loses the point. (Rule 18(e).)

Case 5. A cuts the ball just over the net, and it returns to A's side. B, unable to reach the ball, throws his racket and hits the ball. Both racket and ball fall over the net on A's court. A returns the ball outside of B's court. Does B win or lose the point?

Decision. B loses the point. (Rule 18(e) and (h).)

Case 6. A player standing outside the service court is struck by the service ball before it has touched the ground. Does he win or lose the point?

Decision. The player struck loses the point. (Rule 18(g), except as provided under Rule 13(a).)

Case 7. A player standing outside the court volleys the ball or catches it in his hand and claims the point because the ball was certainly going out of court.

Decision. In no circumstance can he claim the point:

(1) If he catches the ball he loses the point under Rule 18(g).

(2) If he volleys it and makes a bad return he loses the point under Rule 18(c).

(3) If he volleys it and makes a good return, the rally continues.

Rule 19

Player Hinders Opponent

If a player commits any act either deliberate or involuntary which, in the opinion of the Umpire, hinders his opponent in making a stroke, the Umpire shall in the first case award the point to the opponent, and in the second case order the point to be re-played.

Case 1. Is a player liable to a penalty if in making a stroke he touches his opponent?

Decision. No, unless the Umpire deems it necessary to take action under Rule 19.

Case 2. When a ball bounds back over the net, the player concerned may reach over the net in order to play the ball. What is the ruling if the player is hindered from doing this by his opponent?

Decision. In accordance with Rule 19, the Umpire may either award the point to the player hindered, or order the point to be re-played. (See also Rule 23.)

Rule 20

Ball Falling on Line—Good

A ball falling on a line is regarded as falling in the Court bounded by that line.

Rule 21

Ball Touching Permanent Fixture

If the ball in play touch a permanent fixture (other than the net, posts, cord or metal cable, strap or band) after it has hit the ground, the player who struck it wins the point; if before it hits the ground his opponent wins the point.

Case 1. A return hits the Umpire or his chair or stand. The player claims that the ball was going into court.

Decision. He loses the point.

Rule 22

Good Return

It is a good return:

(a) If the ball touch the net, posts, cord or metal cable, strap or band, provided that it passes over any of them and hits the ground within the Court; or
(b) If the ball, served or returned, hit the ground within the proper Court and rebound or be blown back over the net, and the player whose turn it is to strike reach over the net and play the ball, provided that neither he nor any part of his clothes or racket touch the net, posts, cord or metal cable, strap or band or the ground within his opponent's Court, and that the stroke be otherwise good; or
(c) If the ball be returned outside the post, either above or below the level of the top of the net, even though it touch the post, provided that it hits the ground within the proper Court; or
(d) If a player's racket pass over the net after he has returned the ball, provided the ball pass the net before being played and be properly returned; or
(e) If a player succeed in returning the ball, served or in play, which strikes a ball lying in the Court.

Note.—If in a singles match, for the sake of convenience, a doubles court be equipped with singles posts for the purpose of a singles game, then the doubles posts and those portions of the net, cord or metal cable and band outside such singles posts shall at all times be permanent fixtures, and are not regarded as posts or parts of the net of a singles game.

A return that passes under the net cord between the singles and adjacent doubles post without touching either net cord, net or doubles post and falls within the area of play, is a good return.

Case 1. A ball going out of court hits a net post and falls within the lines of the opponent's court. Is the stroke good?

Decision. If a service; no, under Rule 9(c). If other than a service; yes, under Rule 22(a).

Case 2. Is it a good return if a player returns the ball holding his racket in both hands?

Decision. Yes.

Case 3. The Service, or ball in play, strikes a ball lying in the court. Is the point won or lost thereby?

Decision. No. Play must continue. If it is not clear to the Umpire that the right ball is returned a let should be called.

Case 4. May a player use more than one racket at any time during play?

Decision. No: the whole implication of the rules is singular.

Case 5. May a player request that a ball or balls lying in his opponent's court be removed?

Decision. Yes, but not while a ball is in play.

Rule 23

Interference

In case a player is hindered in making a stroke by anything not within his control except a permanent fixture of the Court, or except as provided for in Rule 19, the point shall be re-played.

Case 1. A spectator gets into the way of a player, who fails to return the ball. May the player then claim a let?

Decision. Yes, if in the Umpire's opinion he was obstructed by circumstances beyond his control, but not if due to permanent fixtures of the Court or the arrangements of the ground.

Case 2. A player is interfered with as in Case No. 1, and the Umpire calls a let. The Server had previously served a fault. Has he the right to two services?

Decision. Yes; as the ball is in play, the point, not merely the stroke must be re-played as the rule provides.

Case 3. May a player claim a let under Rule 23 because he thought his opponent was being hindered, and consequently did not expect the ball to be returned?

Decision. No.

Case 4. Is a stroke good when a ball in play hits another ball in the air?

Decision. A let should be called unless the other ball is in the air by the act of one of the players, in which case the Umpire will decide under Rule 19.

Case 5. If an Umpire or other judge erroneously calls "fault" or "out," and then corrects himself and calls "play," which of the calls shall prevail?

Decision. A let must be called, unless, in the opinion of the Umpire, neither player was hindered in his game, in which case the corrected call shall prevail.

Case 6. If the first ball served—a fault—rebounds, interfering with the Receiver at the time of the second service, may the Receiver claim a let?

Decision. Yes. But if he had an opportunity to remove the ball from the court and negligently failed to do so, he may not claim a let.

Case 7. Is it a good stroke if the ball touches a stationary or moving object on the court?

Decision. It is a good stroke unless the stationary object came into court after the ball was put into play in which case a "let" must be called. If the ball in play strikes an object moving along or above the surface of the court a "let" must be called.

Case 8. What is the ruling if the first service is a fault, the second service correct, and it becomes necessary to call a let either under the provision of Rule 23 or if the Umpire is unable to decide the point?

Decision. The fault shall be annulled and the whole point re-played.

Rule 24

The Game

If a player wins his first point, the score is called *15* for that player; on winning his second point, the score is called *30* for that player; on winning his third point, the score is called *40* for that player, and the fourth point won by a player is scored *game* for that player except as below:

If both players have won three points, the score is called *deuce;* and the next point won by a player is called *advantage* for that player. If the same player wins the next point, he wins the game; if the other player wins the next point the score is again called *deuce;* and so on until a player wins the two points immediately following the score at deuce, when the game is scored for that player.

Rule 25

The Set

A player (or players) who first wins six games wins a set; except that he must win by a margin of at least two games over his opponent and where necessary a set shall be extended until this margin be achieved.

Rule 26

When Players Change Sides

The players shall change sides at the end of the first, third and every subsequent alternate game of each set, and at the end of each set unless the total number of games in such set be even, in which case the change is not made until the end of the first game of the next set.

Rule 27

Maximum Number of Sets

The maximum number of sets in a match shall be 5, or, where women take part, 3.

Rule 28

Rules Apply to Both Sexes

Except where otherwise stated, every reference in these Rules to the masculine includes the feminine gender.

Rule 29

Decisions of Umpire and Referee

In matches where an Umpire is appointed, his decision shall be final; but where a Referee is appointed, an appeal shall lie to him from the decision of an Umpire on a question of law, and in all such cases the decision of the Referee shall be final.

The Referee, in his discretion, may at any time postpone a match on account of darkness or the condition of the ground or the weather. In any case of postponement the previous score and previous occupancy of Courts shall hold good, unless the Referee and the players unanimously agree otherwise.

Rule 30

Play shall be continuous from the first service till the match be concluded; provided that after the third set, or when women take part, the second set, either player is entitled to a rest, which shall not exceed 10 minutes, or in countries situated between Latitude 15 degrees North and Latitude 15 degrees South, 45 minutes, and provided further that when necessitated by circumstances not within the control of the players, the Umpire may suspend play for such a period as he may consider necessary. If play be suspended and be not resumed until a later day the rest may be taken only after the third set (or when women take part the second set) of play on such later day, completion of an unfinished set being counted as one set. These provisions shall be strictly construed, and play shall never be suspended, delayed or interfered with for the purpose of enabling a player to recover his strength or his wind, or to receive instruction or advice. The Umpire shall be the sole judge of such suspension, delay or interference, and after giving due warning he may disqualify the offender.

Note.—Any Nation is at liberty to modify the first provision of Rule 30, or omit it from its regulations governing tournaments, matches or competitions held in its own country, other than the International Lawn Tennis Championship (Davis Cup).

Explanation. In men's events there is no rest in a two out of three set match, but in a three out of five set match, a ten-minute rest may be taken only after the third set. It may not be taken before the third set or at any time after the fourth set has been started. It must be taken after the third set or not at all.

In women's matches a rest of ten minutes may be taken after the second set or not at all.

All matches for Juniors shall be the best two out of three sets with no rest. In the case of Tennis Center Championships or Interscholastic, State and Sectional Tournaments, equivalent to Tennis Centers, and in National Junior Championships the final round shall be the best three out of five sets. If such final requires more than three sets to decide, THERE MUST BE a rest of ten minutes after the third set.

Matches for Boys and Girls 15 shall be the best two out of three sets and there must be a ten-minute rest after the second set.

The United States Lawn Tennis Association has approved a modification of the first provision in Rule 30 to provide after the second set in tournaments exclusively for Seniors and in tournaments for Fathers and Sons, either player or doubles team is entitled to a rest which shall not exceed ten minutes.

The players must be back on the court ten minutes after play has ceased.

Should a player, on account of physical unfitness or an unavoidable accident, not within his control, be unable to continue play, he must be defaulted.

"Stalling" is one of the hardest things to deal with. The rules say that "play shall be continuous." An Umpire should determine whether the "stalling" is *deliberate and for the purpose of gaining time. If he decides that it is, he should warn the player to stop his unfair practice. If this does not end it, he should then default him.*

The Umpire has the power to suspend a match for such period as he may think necessary, if, in his judgment, the play is interfered with by circumstances beyond the players' control. Such circumstances might be the passing of an airplane, moving of spectators in the stands, etc.

Case 1. A player's clothing, footwear, or equipment becomes out of adjustment in such a way that it is impossible or undesirable for him to play on. May play be suspended while the maladjustment is rectified?

Decision. If this occurs in circumstances not within the control of the player, of which circumstances the Umpire is the sole judge, a suspension may be allowed.

Case 2. If, owing to an accident, a player is unable to continue immediately, is there any limit to the time during which play may be suspended?

Decision. No allowance may be made for natural loss of physical condition. Consideration may be given by the Umpire for accidental loss of physical ability or condition.

Case 3. During a doubles game, may one of the partners leave the court while the ball is in play?

Decision. Yes, so long as the Umpire is satisfied that play is continuous within the meaning of the rules, and that there is no conflict with Rules 33 and 34.

THE DOUBLES GAME
Rule 31

The above Rules shall apply to the Doubles Game except as below.

Rule 32

Dimensions of Court

For the Doubles Game, the Court shall be 36 feet in width, i.e., 4½ feet wider on each side than the Court for the Singles Game, and those portions of the singles side-lines which lie between the two service-lines shall be called the service-side-lines. In other respects, the Court shall be similar to that described in Rule 1, but the portions of the singles side-lines between the base-line and service-line on each side of the net may be omitted if desired.

Case 1. In doubles the Server claims the right to stand at the corner of the court as marked by the doubles side-line. Is the foregoing correct or is it necessary that the Server stand within the limits of the center mark and the singles side-line?

Decision. The Server has the right to stand anywhere between the center mark and the double side-lines.

Rule 33

Order of Service

The order of serving shall be decided at the beginning of each set as follows:

The pair who have to serve in the first game of each set shall decide which partner shall do so and the opposing pair shall decide similarly for the second game. The partner of the player who served in the first game shall serve in the third: the partner of the player who served in the second game shall serve in the fourth, and so on in the same order in all the subsequent games of a set.

Case 1. In doubles, one player does not appear in time to play, and his partner claims to be allowed to play single-handed against the opposing players. May he do so?

Decision. No.

Rule 34

Order of Receiving

The order of receiving the service shall be decided at the beginning of each set as follows:

The pair who have to receive the service in the first game shall decide which partner shall receive the first service, and that partner shall continue to receive the first service in every odd game throughout that set. The opposing pair shall likewise decide which partner shall receive the first service in the second game and that partner shall continue to receive the first service in every even game throughout that set. Partners shall receive the service alternately throughout each game.

Explanation of Rule 34

The receiving formation of a doubles team may not be changed during a set; only at the start of a new set. Partners must receive throughout each set on the same sides of the court which they originally select when the set begins. The first Server is not required to receive in the right court; he may select either side, but must hold this to the end of the set.

Case 1. Is it allowable in doubles for the server's partner to stand in a position that obstructs the view of the receiver?

Decision. Yes. The server's partner may take any position on his side of the net in or out of the court that he wishes.

Rule 35

Service Out of Turn

If a partner serve out of his turn, the partner who ought to have served shall serve as soon as the mistake is discovered, but all points scored, and any faults served before such discovery, shall be reckoned. If a game shall have been completed before such discovery, the order of service remains as altered.

Rule 36

Error in Order of Receiving

If during a game the order of receiving the service is changed by the receivers it shall remain as altered until the end of the game in which the mistake is discovered, but the partners shall resume their original order of receiving in the next game of that set in which they are receivers of the service.

Rule 37

Ball Touching Server's Partner Is Fault

The service is a fault as provided for by Rule 9, or if the ball served touch the Server's partner or anything he wears or carries, but if the ball served touch the partner of the Receiver or anything which he wears or carries, not being a let under Rule 13(a), before it hits the ground, the Server wins the point.

Rule 38

Ball Struck Alternately

The ball shall be struck alternately by one or other player of the opposing pairs, and if a player touches the ball in play with his racket in contravention of this Rule, his opponents win the point.

Should any point arise upon which you find it difficult to give a decision or on which you are in doubt as to the proper ruling, immediately write, giving full details, to the Tennis Umpires Association, care of U.S.L.T.A., 120 Broadway, New York City 10005, and full instructions and explanations will be sent you.

GLOSSARY

Band	The strip of canvas attached to the top of the net.
Base line	The back line at either end of the court.
Center mark	The mark bisecting the base line, defining one of the limits of the service position.
Center service line	The line dividing the service court into halves and separating the right and left service courts.
Change-of-length	Shots that are made with varying lengths; one deep; followed by one short.
Change-of-pace	Shots made with varying speed; one fast; one slow.
Cross-court shot	A stroke hit across to the opposite side of center from which it is hit.
Down-the-line shot	A stroke hit down the side line from the same side of center from which it is hit.
Drop shot	A stroke that is made after the ball has bounced and hit with underspin to land short on the other side of the net.
Drop volley	A shot hit on the fly before the ball has bounced to make it land short on the other side of the net.
Fault	A served ball that does not strike in the proper court, or is not properly served.
Foot fault	Position or movements of the feet before or during the service in violation of Rule 6.
Game	The unit of scoring next higher than the point; scored when either side has won four points, unless the other side has meantime won three; in that case the side first gaining a lead of two points wins.
Ground stroke	A shot hit after it has bounced.
Half volley (or pickup)	A shot hit just barely after it has hit the ground.
Let	A served ball that touches the net and yet goes into the proper court. Also any stroke that does not count and is played over.
Linesman	An official of the match, whose duties are defined in the Regulations.
Lob	A stroke which hits a ball high in the air.
Net	The netting placed across the middle of the court.

171

Passing shot	A stroke that is hit, which passes your opponent at the net.
Permanent fixtures	The Umpire, Linesmen and spectators and their chairs or stands, net, posts, back and sidestops, and any other objects situated around the court. (Also see note to Playing Rule No. 2.)
In play	A ball is "in play" from the moment at which it is delivered in service until the point has been decided.
Point	The smallest unit of the score. Four points scored win a game, unless both sides have won three points, when the score is "deuce" and one side must gain a lead of two points to win the game.
Post	One of the wooden or metal uprights supporting the net.
Racket	The implement used to strike the ball.
Receiver	The player who receives the service.
Referee	The official in charge of a tournament, whose duties are defined in the Regulations.
Running-in shot	A stroke made and followed to the net.
To serve	To put the ball into play.
Server	The player who serves.
Service, or serve	The act of putting the ball into play.
Service line	The line 21 feet from the net that bounds the back of the service courts.
Set	The unit of scoring next higher than the game; scored when either side has won six games, unless the other side has meantime won five; in that case the side first gaining a lead of two games wins.
Side line	The line at either side of the court that marks the outside edge of the playing surface.
Side service line	The line forming the boundary of the service courts at the right and left sides. In singles the side service lines are also part of the side lines.
Stroke	The act of striking the ball with the racket.
Toss	To spin or throw up the racket for choice of service court.
Tournament	An official competition.
Umpire	The official in charge of the match whose duties are defined in the Regulations.
Volley	A stroke made by hitting a ball before it has touched the ground, except in serving.

USEFUL INFORMATION

For the best information concerning equipment; instruction articles; club activities; tennis camps and resorts; sectional, national and international tournaments, including schedules and results etc., write to "World Tennis," 8100 Westglen, Houston, Texas 77042. This magazine is published monthly—rate $6.00 per year.

For an excellent reference book, write to the United States Lawn Tennis Association, 51 East 42nd St., New York City 10005, and ask for its "Official U.S.L.T.A. Yearbook and Tennis Guide," which is published annually at a cost of $3.00 per copy. It is extremely well indexed and contains a tremendous amount of background material, including records of past and present players and events.